Progressive Rock Drumming

A Guide to Playing and Creating Innovative [...] in Various Progressive Rock Sty[...]

By Dan Maske

To access audio visit:
www.halleonard.com/mylibrary

Enter Code
5686-6751-9944-1922

Edited by Rick Mattingly

ISBN 978-1-4234-3361-3

HAL•LEONARD®
CORPORATION

7777 W. BLUEMOUND RD. P.O. BOX 13819 MILWAUKEE, WI 53213

In Australia Contact:
Hal Leonard Australia Pty. Ltd.
4 Lentara Court
Cheltenham, Victoria, 3192 Australia
Email: ausadmin@halleonard.com.au

Visit Hal Leonard Online at
www.halleonard.com

Contents

About the Author

Dan Maske is an award-winning composer, performer, teacher, and author. His progressive rock band, Far Corner (Far-corner.com), has released two albums on Cuneiform Records (Cuneiformrecords.com) and has performed throughout the Midwest and elsewhere, including progressive rock festivals such as ProgDay (Chapel Hill, N.C.) and the Orion Sound Studios Progressive Rock Showcase (Baltimore, Md.). A third album is expected to be released in 2014. Maske founded the band with his wife, Angela Schmidt, who plays cello in the group.

Besides Maske's involvement with progressive rock, Dan composes orchestral and chamber music that has been performed around the world. In addition to his experience as a drummer, he is also a pianist, trumpet player, and conductor. Maske holds B.A. and M.M. degrees in music theory/composition from the University of Wisconsin-Milwaukee, and a doctorate in music composition from the University of Wisconsin-Madison. He teaches music composition for the Milwaukee Youth Symphony Orchestra, and is on the music faculty of Cardinal Stritch University in Milwaukee, Wisconsin. Visit Danielmaske.com for more information.

Recording Credits

Drumset, keyboards, and composition: Dan Maske

Guitars: Sean Gill

Bass: Tom McGirr

Music Recorded and Produced by Dan Maske at Corner Labs, Wisconsin

Introduction

Musical Notation

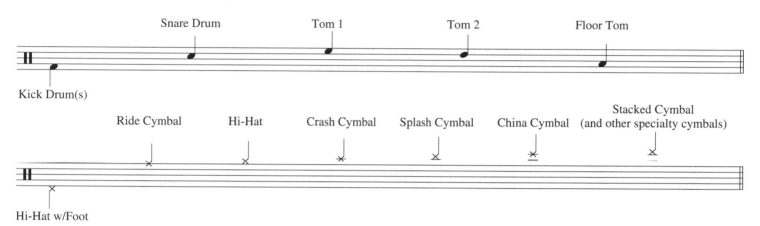

Open hi-hat notes should be immediately followed by closing the hi-hat with the foot. It is most effective and easiest to execute this when it is done at the same time as the next note played by the hands. The following notation shows the closing of the hi-hat with the foot.

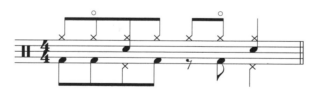

However, to avoid an unnecessarily complicated rhythmic notation, this will rarely be notated in subsequent examples. Simply get in the habit of closing the hi-hat with the foot as you play the next note with the hands.

Ghost notes are played very lightly, often on the snare drum, but may be utilized on any drum or cymbal. For the purposes of this book, please refer to the following notational guidelines regarding ghost notes:

When ghost notes are called for, non-ghost notes will be marked with an accent. In these cases, all notes on that drum that do not carry an accent should be played as ghost notes. This only applies to one measure at a time; in other words, when a measure has both accented and unaccented snare drum notes, in the subsequent measure, the notes—if not marked with an accent—should be played as regular notes (not ghost notes). Also, accents only apply to that particular drum; in a bar with unaccented and accented snare drum notes, any notes played on a tom should be played as regular notes unless some tom notes have accents. In cases where *all* notes within a measure on a particular drum are to be played as ghost notes, there will be no accents to signify that these are supposed to be ghosted; therefore, a special instruction will be placed above the staff. When in doubt, refer to the recording. And since notation is not meant to be taken literally in every detail (although in an instruction book, it should come close), you should use your own discretion and artistic instinct when it comes to interpreting and playing the notated examples. If something sounds good to you, do it.

Sticking (R, L) is indicated sparsely throughout the book. It is usually included in trickier passages where a specific sticking may save you time in practicing an example, and where there is only one sticking pattern that keeps the drumset part from being very awkward to play.

Full band scores are provided for many of the examples. This includes a grand staff (two staves connected by a brace, as in piano music) with keyboards on the top staff and guitar (stems up) and bass (stems down) on the bottom staff. In some cases, the guitar may be notated on the top staff when it helps provide for a less cluttered score. When this is done, a note in the score indicates it. Also, not all details played by these instruments are always included in the scores. The notation includes the important tracks that define the music, but in some cases, "overdubs" (additional notes beyond the basic parts, those that a live band may not be able to execute without the need of additional musicians) have not been included. In this book, overdubs are usually present in the keyboard part to enhance orchestration.

Because this is a drumset book, the drumset staff has been placed on top with the keyboards/guitar/bass underneath, even though percussion would normally be included on a lower staff. In cases where a particular example includes an instrument that does not play, that staff has been eliminated for that example.

Thus, the instrument staves are not labeled, as this score arrangement is consistent throughout the book.

About the Audio

Count-offs have been included at the start of every track. Although count-offs are commonly reserved for play-along tracks and not demo tracks, they may help listeners establish the tempo in their minds clearly so that when the drumset example begins, they are prepared and can better digest the example on the first hearing, even though multiple listenings may be beneficial and are recommended.

Almost all examples have been recorded using a real band featuring keyboards, acoustic and electric guitars, bass, and drumset in an attempt to put all drumming concepts in the context of a full progressive rock ensemble.

About Progressive Rock

The Introduction discusses characteristics of various progressive rock subgenres, but a few introductory comments are also provided here. In the twenty-first century, progressive rock is alive and well. Thanks to the Internet and recording technology, the style has seen a renaissance since the 1990s. There are literally thousands of prog rock groups around the world, made more possible by the ability to record albums inexpensively as well as market and distribute them without the need of a major record label.

While the world of progressive rock is filled with many creative and skilled drummers, they owe much of their craft to a handful of drummers from the early history of the style. Some of the most notable, covering a variety of prog rock subgenres, include Neil Peart of Rush; Bill Bruford of Yes and King Crimson; Terry Bozzio, who played with Frank Zappa (and countless other prog rock projects); and a bit more recently (since the mid to late 1980s), Mike Portnoy of Dream Theater. While this sampling represents some of the most popular progressive rock, there are other influential drummers whose popularity exists in cult status; they may not have achieved wide mainstream success, but are no less innovative or impacting on the world of adventurous drumming.

Progressive rock requires the ability to play, know, and understand a variety of disparate musical styles—not just poplar music styles such as rock and jazz, but also classical music (particularly classical music from the twentieth century) and folk music from around the world. Knowledge of these styles, in addition to basic rock drumming techniques, has helped define progressive rock drumming. Knowing the most basic type of rock beat and being able to make it groove as it would in the best rock 'n' roll is just as important as being skilled and familiar with percussion techniques used in some of the most adventurous and complex contemporary "classical" works of the twentieth and twenty-first centuries.

However, since many of the founding progressive rock drummers drew on these different styles of music, their drumming produced a style in which these varied types of music have been combined in different proportions, creating a new style (with many variations) that is possible for current drummers to emulate. This means that a young drummer today doesn't necessarily have to possess great familiarity with classical and world music in order to create drumset parts and play in a way that is inclusive of these styles of music. In learning from some of the founding drummers of progressive rock, you will be taking on a second-hand, but effective knowledge of other styles of music. Still, it can help you develop your own unique drumming voice to explore many different types of music—even music that does not include drumset or any percussion at all—and you are encouraged to do so.

While this book mentions other styles of music, it is not a detailed study of these styles and how they manifest themselves in progressive rock drumming. It is a look at many of the techniques used by the founding prog drummers and an instruction in how you can create your own drumset parts based on these techniques. And because even a small number of basic techniques can produce infinite possibilities in creating drumset parts, as well as the fact that some of the most famous prog rock drummers create and play in very different ways from each other, one other facet of this book is that it shows how multiple and very different drumset parts can be created for the same music.

Some may believe progressive rock drumming to be characterized by a certain showy busyness. But while that might be a part of some of the music, what also sets prog rock drumming apart from other rock music is its inventiveness, using outside-the-box techniques and compositional choices that help make the style into the unique and adventurous music it is. One need not overplay, show off in a constant display of technical prowess, or make use of a drumkit of monstrous size in order to be unique and interesting and sound "proggy." While this book will indeed explore some techniques that may be used to show off due to the technical demands, it will also instruct the reader on how to create original and inventive drumset parts without the need to play in a demanding virtuosic style. In addition, all of what is demonstrated in this book can be played on a standard five-piece drumset with a basic set of cymbals (hi-hats, ride, crash, and Chinese cymbals, with some expansion into splash and "stacked" cymbal combinations).

■ *Chapter 1*
WHAT IS PROGRESSIVE ROCK?

Progressive rock is a style of rock music that began in the late 1960s. Using the Beatles' 1967 *Sgt. Pepper's Lonely Hearts Club Band* album as a foundation, many musicians began to push the boundaries of rock music. Part of this push came in the form of applying classical music forms and virtuosity to the compositions; longer songs, mood changes, surprises, and a certain element of drama set this style apart from rock 'n' roll. This music existed more for the true listening experience, rather than serving the role of music for dancing, partying, and rebellion. Lyrics were often about subjects other than love and socializing, and took on science fiction, fantasy, and philosophical themes.

Many consider the first true progressive rock album to be *In the Court of the Crimson King*, the 1969 album from King Crimson. Other founding groups that began around the same time include Yes; Emerson, Lake & Palmer (ELP); Genesis; and Jethro Tull. More bands soon followed, such as Gentle Giant, Kansas, and Rush. These groups attained high levels of popularity and are probably the best known. However, many other groups from all over the world had their beginnings in the early '70s, and many new progressive rock bands continue to form, record, and perform—all of which are in no small part responsible for the phenomenon of the genre.

Progressive Rock Subgenres

Over the years, the progressive rock genre branched out into many different styles referred to as "subgenres." Though the subgenres below are quite clearly defined, one may notice some overlap. No artist simply belongs to only one of these categories, but often combine qualities of several. Prevalent in all progressive rock is a desire to move beyond the accepted mainstream of popular music and draw heavily upon other styles, all under a "rock" umbrella. Though classical music may dominate as an influence in a large number of groups, many styles from all over the world play a part. The terms below are only some of the most common subgenre labels. There are many more. For a complete listing with thorough descriptions, visit *The Gibraltar Encyclopedia of Progressive Rock* online at www.gepr.net.

Some of the artists listed below could easily be placed under a different subgenre. However, for the sake of this book, they have been listed under the subgenre they are most commonly associated with today. To better understand how these subgenres sound, you must listen to the artists—those listed here as well as the countless others with bodies of work to explore.

Symphonic

Most of the founding progressive rock bands from the late 1960s to early '70s fall under this category. The term "symphonic" refers to elements such as the use of orchestral instruments and keyboards simulating a large symphonic sound. Classical music forms come into play, with single songs spanning durations above twenty minutes, and some songs existing as multi-movement works in a direct parallel to classical music. Displays of musical virtuosity are also common in the form of demanding solos, meter changes, shifts in tempo, and mood changes. Some music consists of an expansion and development of the pop-rock song. These tunes contained the catchy hooks prevalent in pop music, but sought to develop these hooks and themes further, both instrumentally and vocally. Though the subgenre saw its heyday in the 1970s, many groups continued in the style, with a renaissance of new bands appearing in the 1990s. Notable founding artists include Yes, Genesis, ELP, King Crimson, PFM, and Banco. Some newer bands include Spock's Beard, Änglagård, and The Flower Kings.

Classical

This subgenre may be seen as an overlap, or perhaps a more specific focus on an area of symphonic. One of the more distinguishing characteristics includes a stronger, more direct imitation of the compositional techniques found in classical music. The term "classical," as used in this case, refers more specifically to music before 1900, encompassing the Baroque, Classical, and Romantic periods. Classical music as it was in the twentieth century is often compared to progressive rock in the "Rock in Opposition" subgenre (see below); however, the trend of using odd and changing meters, a twentieth-century classical convention, is a hallmark characteristic across progressive rock in all subgenres.

In this classical prog style, music could often sound like that of Mozart, for example, played on rock music instruments. Sometimes, as in the case of ELP, a group would take actual classical compositions and arrange them for rock band. Notable artists include The Nice, ELP, Gentle Giant, Ekseption, and Ars Nova.

Fusion

Often called "jazz rock," fusion is more a subgenre of jazz than progressive rock, with its beginnings stemming from Miles Davis's *Bitches Brew*. Occasionally, when the classical music influence is particularly strong in the construction of the tunes, fusion is referred to as a part of progressive rock, rather than jazz, though this usage is ambiguous. The music is largely based on improvised soloing, but includes more composed elements than most jazz. Prominent artists include Soft Machine, Nucleus, Brand X, Niacin, Allan Holdsworth, Mahavishnu Orchestra, Tribal Tech, Tunnels, and Return to Forever.

Neo-Progressive

Neo-progressive came about in the early '80s, evolving from the more pop-directed sound of late-'70s Genesis. By this time, the early- to mid-'70s progressive rock styles had faded from the mainstream, with most of the genre going underground. This "new" progressive rock still possessed some of the characteristics of the earlier prog, but it was more refined and polished, with a bigger emphasis on hook-driven song structures. Thus, this subgenre is considered to be the most "audience friendly," often bordering on being pop music and not concerned with breaking ground or going to any extremes. One may think of it as progressive-influenced pop rock. Some of the bands from the '70s evolved into a neo-progressive style in the '80s in order to keep up with the times and survive. Bands adopting this idiom include Collage, IQ, Jadis, Marillion, Pallas, Pendragon, and some Rush ('80s–'00s).

Progressive Metal

Progressive metal saw its birth in the 1980s as heavy and speed metal (thrash) stylings combined with some influences from the classic '70s bands. Bands with a heavier edge like Rush and Deep Purple, along with metal groups like Metallica and Iron Maiden, were of great influence. What often sets progressive metal apart from standard metal is the use of keyboards, complex counterpoint, and extensive use of changing meters. Notable artists include Dream Theater, Fates Warning, Symphony X, Ayreon, Shadow Gallery, and Pain of Salvation.

Other groups such as Rush and, more recently, Porcupine Tree, take on some characteristics of metal, but are more difficult to include in the "progressive metal" category. They possess some of the guitar-heavy riffs and double-kick drumming associated with the subgenre, but these may either be taken to a less extreme level or used a bit more sparingly. These groups (as with many bands) could be included in many or even all of the other subgenre categories, and are only listed here because they, Rush especially, have been highly influential on many prog metal bands, especially in the world of drumming.

Rock in Opposition (RIO)

The term "Rock in Opposition" comes from an organizational movement by five European bands in the late '70s. The "opposition" in this case was to the music industry's demands of compromise over art. These bands chose to create music they were proud of, without regard to marketability—no trying to guess what the public wanted. They were out to write and record music, not commercial products. Thus, the music was often adventurous, extending far beyond traditions and conventions of mainstream rock. Compositions covered a wide range in styles from contemporary classical music to avant-garde experimentalism. Eventually the movement disbanded, but the term "RIO" persisted, representing the most adventurous side of progressive rock. The original RIO bands were Henry Cow, Univers Zero, Samla Mammas Manna, Stormy Six, and Etron Fou. Next-generation RIO-style bands include Thinking Plague, 5UUs, Sleepytime Gorilla Museum, and Miriodor.

Space Rock

Born in the '60s from the psychedelic stylings of early Pink Floyd, space rock's primary focus is on creating atmosphere. Part of the goal was to create music for sitting down and listening—as opposed to music for dancing, à la rock 'n' roll. This notion played a heavy role in the spawning of progressive rock, which attempted to create "concert works" for listening to, akin to classical music. The difference with space rock was its emphasis on hallucinogenic and surreal imagery, with listening being more of a relaxing, meditative experience. While some of the music may be soothing and relaxing, other compositions take a more aggressive approach, full of great tension and drama. Heavy use of effects such as delay and reverb are a major part of the spacey sound. Synthesizers representing non-acoustic instruments also play an important role. In addition to Pink Floyd, noteworthy groups include Gong, Hawkwind, Ozric Tentacles, Hidria Spacefolk, Ship of Fools, and Quarkspace.

Summary

In the spirit of progessiveness, this book discusses and presents examples from each subgenre above. So whether you wish to create a big symphonic sound, improvise some tasty solos, add a classical music spice to your playing, forge blistering heavy metal lines, concoct some spacey sonic constellations, or all of the above, you'll be provided with the tools to accomplish these goals.

Drumming Styles in Progressive Rock

Chapters two and three will explore drumming elements that set progressive rock apart from other types of rock music. These chapters will also discuss drumming techniques that may characterize and distinguish various subgenres within progressive rock, as multiple drumset interpretations are presented for the same tune. But instead of attaching specific techniques or entire drumset parts to individual progressive rock subgenres, these elements may be considered as belonging to any and all stylistic categories. When one technique or drumset beat or phrase is strongly indicative of one subgenre, an effort will be made to mention such a connection to better inform drummers reading this book who wish to hone their creative technique within the confines of one of these sub styles (i.e., if they are playing in a prog metal band in which all band members wish for the drumming to be as strongly characteristic of that particular style as possible).

Chapter 2
BASIC PROGRESSIVE TECHNIQUES

This chapter presents some drumming techniques common to a lot of progressive rock. With regular practice of these techniques, progressive drummers can build up a library of motives and gestures that will become second nature, thereby allowing them to incorporate them into their overall playing and compositional style. Some may be simple and others more complex, but all techniques take the percussionist beyond what is considered traditional rock drumming, even though they may not be completely unique to progressive rock. Also, there are many more techniques that may constitute progressive drumming, but they will be discussed on a case-by-case basis. In some examples in the Songs chapter, it will be up to you to listen to, study, and practice the parts in order to discover additional techniques that may be more nuanced than what gets mentioned here. Just as you would when listening to your favorite prog rock music, listen to the music provided online and make your own observations beyond what is pointed out in the text. This is how you will learn and develop your own unique style.

The techniques in this chapter focus on what may be considered the largest drumming concepts with respect to how prevalent they are in prog, or the fact that they are "umbrella" categories, which may include a variety of possibilities underneath them. In addition, compositional choices on the part of the drummer will often rely upon what the other instruments are doing. Some of these choices may be discussed in this book, and others you must observe on your own. Experienced drummers may not always be consciously aware of every little nuanced technique they are employing, even when being asked to explain a drumset part they have created. And so to help you make your own observations—not only as to what techniques are being employed (and what makes the drumset parts sound "progressive"), but why they have been chosen by the author—full band scores have been included with many of the examples in this chapter and all examples in the Songs chapter so you can both see and hear what the other instruments are doing and how they work as a whole.

The techniques presented here may be expanded upon, including combining multiple techniques into one beat. In this chapter, you are encouraged to listen to the audio tracks, play the examples, and then create some of your own beats using these techniques. In the next chapter, you will be presented with several short songs, each of which includes a "minus-drums" play-along track. Here, you will be able to create your own drumset parts to specific full-band music and play along.

Ride/Hi-Hat Combination

This example shows a basic rock beat, one that is often presented at the very beginning of most drumset methods.

🔊 Ride/Hi-Hat Combination 1

We can enhance this basic beat without changing the basic snare and kick pattern; rather, we'll change the ride and hi-hat. With the right hand playing the ride cymbal and the left hand playing the hi-hat in a specific rhythmic pattern, you can create a more interesting variation on a basic rock beat. But such rhythmic patterns may also be created and employed because they reflect rhythms being played in the guitar, bass, or keyboards.

The next example enhances the basic rock beat with a new rhythmic pattern between the ride and hi-hat (the snare and kick drum notes remain the same).

Ride/Hi-Hat Combination 2

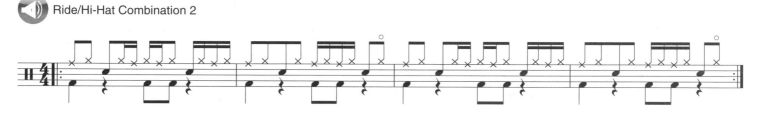

Exactly what kind of pattern you create for the hands may depend on what the other instruments are doing. The next example takes the same beat, but now played with guitar and bass. You can see the parts notated and understand how they fit together. Listening to the audio track will also demonstrate how the two complement each other.

Ride/Hi-Hat Combination 3

If the song was a progressive metal tune, you could enhance this beat with some steady double kick to bring out a heavier feel. In the next example, also note the splash cymbal instead of hi-hat on the "and" of beat 4 in the second and fourth bars.

Ride/Hi-Hat Combination 4

There are an endless number of ways to enhance drumset parts using the ride and hi-hat in this fashion. Additional basic as well as advanced methods will be explored later in the book. The following demonstrates one last example making use of this technique with some 7/8 bars mixed in to make it more of a challenge.

Ride/Hi-Hat Combination 5

Off-Beat China Cymbal

This technique is a staple in a much progressive rock. Its earliest and perhaps best-known usage is in the music of Rush.

While use of a standard Chinese cymbal itself may be an identifiable characteristic in a lot of prog, this particular rhythm has been a prog rock drumming staple, especially in progressive hard rock and progressive metal. Most simply, where a ride or hi-hat might play steady eighth notes ("1 and 2 and," etc.), the Chinese cymbal will instead play only on the "and" of every beat. The first two bars of the next example use our basic rock beat and replace the ride/hi-hat with a Chinese cymbal in between each beat. Starting in measure 3, the beat becomes a bit more complex.

🔊 Off-Beat China Cymbal 1

Since this might be a bit tricky at first to some drummers (especially when other elements of the beat are more complex), one method to make it easier is to keep the steady eighth note going as before, but play on each beat with the ride (or hi-hat, depending on where your Chinese cymbal is positioned).

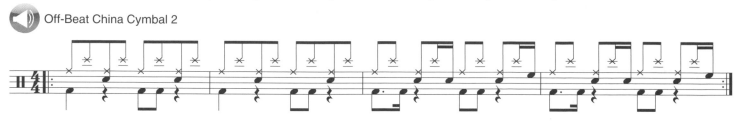

One may also play the ride notes in the air instead, thereby limiting the amount of "noise," allowing the off-beat China effect to be clear.

In addition to the Chinese cymbal, other cymbals with a short decay may be substituted. These include stacked cymbals, which usually involve stacking a small Chinese cymbal ("China Splash") on top of a regular splash cymbal. This sound may be described as having a "trashy" characteristic. And speaking of trashy, actual metal trashcan lids may be used (mounted on cymbal stands) to augment the drumset. Other metallic objects such as ordinary sheet metal and various household or kitchen components may also be mounted on cymbal stands. Drummers in the Avant Progressive subgenre often add to their kits with "found objects" from around the house. The following two tracks use one particular stack combination and sheet metal.

Chinese splash (10-inch) stacked on top of a regular splash (10-inch)

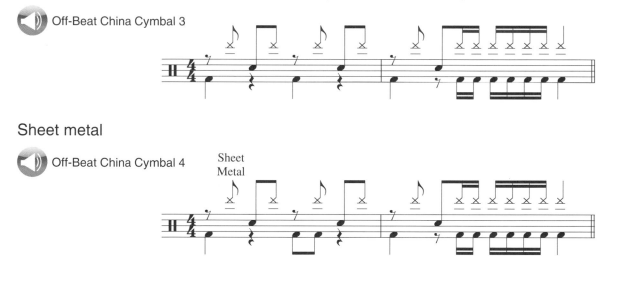

Sheet metal

Linear Playing

The first beats most drummers learn to play involve *keeping time* (steady eighth or sixteenth notes or, in some cases, quarters) on the hi-hat or ride while the kick and snare fill in some sort of backbeat pattern that involves the snare playing on beats two and four (in 4/4 time). This is at the core of basic rock drumming, and the vast majority of rock drummers play around this beat. What results is that multiple limbs will be playing notes at the same time on certain beats within the measure. For example, while the snare drum plays the important backbeat notes on two and four, the hi-hat, playing steady eighth notes, also sounds on beats two and four. If the kick drum is playing "four on the floor," as shown in the next example, then three instruments/limbs are sounding notes on beats two and four. The first example in this chapter illustrates this.

Linear technique involves no two (or more) notes happening at the same time. If we take the first beat in this chapter and attempt to create a linear version, while maintaining its important elements, the following would be one simple choice.

The term "linear" refers, in part, to how this sounds and looks as notation. Harmony occurs when two or more pitches are sounded at the same time; in musical notation, this is represented by vertically stacked notes. A melody is often thought of as one note after another, and to see this on the staff, a melody forms a kind of horizontal line (though "mountainous" in contour). So when a linear drumbeat is notated, you don't see any two or more notes stacked vertically at any point.

To be truly or literally linear, there would be no "verticalities" at all, but while such beats might occur, there might be an exception here or there, making a beat mostly linear. At some point, when enough verticalities are sounded, one might refer to the beat as "quasi linear." But for our purposes, all beats that largely follow this concept will be referred to as "linear."

To take a basic rock beat and remove all verticalities, as in the previous example, can result in something that is pretty bland. It might almost sound like something beginning drummers might play because they lack the coordination to keep steady time with one hand while the other limbs do something different. However, when more complex patterns are played, the results can be adventurous, giving the music a more progressive sound.

The next example shows a linear beat that still puts the hi-hat in the time-keeping role, even though it is playing in between the cracks, so to speak. Note that because no two limbs are playing anywhere at the exact same time, the notation puts hands and feet all in the same "voice" (no separation showing the hands with stems up and feet with stems down). This makes the notation look cleaner and easier to read, as there would be a lot of rests if it were notated using two voices.

🔊 Linear Playing 1

Finally, the next pattern sees a variation on the previous beat, adding a bit of extra syncopation and the toms.

🔊 Linear Playing 2

Linear technique will be explored later in a variety of ways, but for now, get a feel for this method of drumset playing by creating your own beats. Feel free to use any of the drumset components, but remember, the more different components you use, the more your beat might start to sound like a fill. Employing the regularity of a pattern as well as limiting how many different components you use (or at least how often you use them) will help it groove.

Tom-Tom Beats

A beat that sees an abundance of notes on the tom-toms, sometimes referred to as a "jungle beat" (though perhaps with political incorrectness), is a common occurrence in progressive rock. Oftentimes, the snare will play on beats two and four while all other eighth or sixteenth notes are played on the toms.

Tom-Tom Beats 1

Playing the snare on two and four ("backbeats") or even playing the snare at all is not required, but doing so helps establish this as a "beat" and not a fill or solo by keeping it grounded via the repetition. However, even with a backbeat snare, this can get tiring for the listener if it is repeated for too long.

What can help keep a tom-tom beat interesting and sustainable is carefully placed accents. Some might say that a tom-tom beat is "all about the accents." Even a simple pattern consisting of some syncopation can allow for an interesting beat that can be used for an entire verse, chorus, or any whole section of music.

The next two examples rely on the accents. Listen to the track and you will notice that the non-accented notes are played quietly, as ghost notes. Ghost notes are important in order to allow the accented notes to stand out. And the accented notes coincide with the rhythms played in the other instruments.

Tom-Tom Beats 2

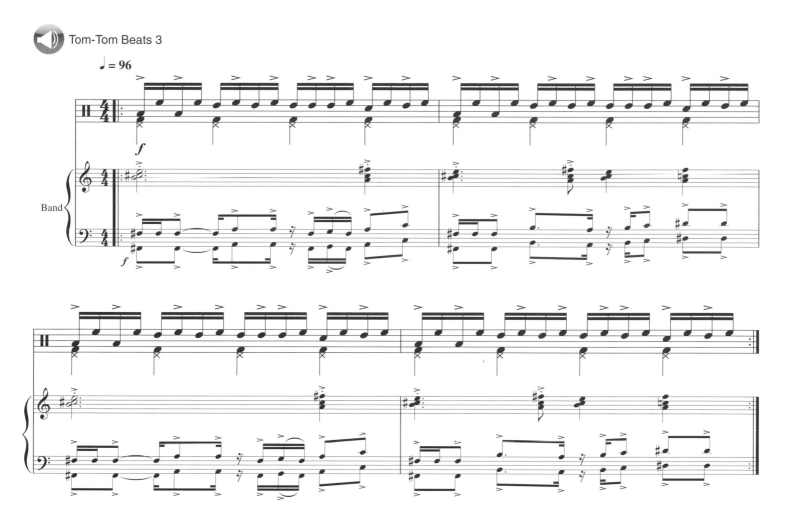

As a drummer, you might create tom-tom beats with syncopated accents because it sounds and feels good to you. You could present such a beat to your band, who might attempt to create a riff to go along with your beat. However, when the band presents some music to you, if you decided to create a tom-tom beat, your accents should reflect the rhythmic feel of the guitar/bass/keys. One way to reflect the rhythmic feel is to highlight the accents in the other instruments (play your accents on the same notes). Another way would be to place your accents somewhere in between the accents of the other instruments, creating a kind of "rhythmic counterpoint."

Metrical and Rhythmic Devices

This heading includes a few subcategories: "Odd and Changing Meter," "Hemiola and Polyrhythms," and "Cross-Rhythms." The first is not necessarily a drumset technique, rather a characteristic of progressive rock that drummers have to deal with. The others can be characteristics of the song as well, but can also involve techniques that a drummer may employ in order to deal with certain rhythmic and metrical elements that characterize a song. All elements have to do with small rhythmic groupings (a measure itself is one kind of rhythmic grouping).

Odd and Changing Meter

One way a band might employ changing meter is to repeat a previous phrase or riff, but in a different meter. The first phrase in the next example sees the guitar riff in 4/4, based on the key of E minor. After this four-bar phrase is played, the guitar moves up in pitch to play a similar riff based on A, but shortened, putting the phrase in 3/4. The drumset plays a four-bar pattern in 4/4 and then a similar pattern in 3/4.

Odd and Changing Meter 1

This represents one way to deal with changing meter while the essential musical material (the guitar riff) remains the same. Besides navigating the meter change, the drumbeat remains the same, but with the variation of the ride cymbal being used instead of hi-hat.

The next example uses the odd meter of 7/8. Usually, such a meter is divided into three groups of eighth notes. For example, 7/8 may consist of the subdivision 2+2+3. One way to think of this is as a measure with three beats: two shorter beats followed by one longer beat. This unevenness makes for what is sometimes referred to as an "asymmetrical meter," and is what makes 7/8 and other odd meters interesting and a bit tricky, especially if your brain is still feeling a more common meter such as 4/4.

Odd and Changing Meter 2

If you're only asked to play a beat in 7/8, you probably have to think about it for a bit and then count it to make sure you have it right. But if you're asked to come up with a 7/8 beat to go along with a guitar part, then by hearing the guitar riff, you can better "feel" the meter because it is directly connected to something musical.

Many times when drummers have to create their own part, they are given at least one part from another instrument. They can listen to the riff, feel it, and then play along, without consciously being aware of what the meter is. It is only afterwards that, when attempting to count, the drummer becomes aware of the meter. The musicality of your drumset part is what matters most, so creating your parts based on how you hear and feel the music can often produce the best results, rather than making it a musical intellectual exercise, seeing how complex you can make your part, especially with respect to playing in the trickier time signatures.

Still, there is nothing wrong with working on your own drumbeats as stand-alone parts first. Doing this can be good for the brain and therefore make for good practice. You may also end up creating something you never would have if you were only coming up with drum parts to accompany some already existing music in other instruments. And if you come up with drumbeats you are proud of, you can always present these to the rest of your group and ask them to compose something to go along with what you've created (or, if you yourself compose music for other instruments, try starting with a drumset part first and then attempt to create guitar, bass, and/or keyboard parts to go along with what you've already created on drumset).

The next example uses both odd and changing meters. Here, the change is between a simple meter of 4/4 and an odd, asymmetrical meter of 7/8. This is fairly common in progressive rock, as the change between these two different types of meters adds an unpredictable character that sounds more complex, keeping the player and the listeners on their toes. In the next example, also note the subtle difference in the drumset part at the end of every other 7/8 measure.

Odd and Changing Meter 3

"Metric modulation" is often present in progressive rock. It is not specifically a drumming technique, rather a compositional element dealing with time, one that progressive drummers should be aware of and learn to navigate. This device was first notably used by twentieth-century classical composer Elliott Carter. In metric modulation, a tempo change occurs by making some kind of note (or note value) in the first tempo equal to a different kind of note in the second tempo. The change often occurs between a compound meter like 6/8 and a simple meter like 4/4. In 6/8, the main pulse (two dotted-quarter-note beats per measure) is divided by three (each dotted-quarter-note pulse is divided by three eighth notes). In 4/4, the main quarter-note pulse is divided by two (two eighth notes per beat). These subdivisions of the beat represent the way a meter is felt.

The following example demonstrates this type of tempo and meter change. The tune begins in 6/8, with a dotted-quarter-note pulse at 112 BPM (beats per minute). In measure 5, the meter changes to 4/4 with a quarter-note-pulse of 84 BPM. In this change, the eighth-note value in the 6/8 measures is equivalent to the sixteenth-note value in the 4/4 measures. Thus, when switching to 4/4, it is like accenting every four notes instead of every three.

Odd and Changing Meter 4

If you were only to hear the eighth notes without accents in the 6/8 measures change to the sixteenth notes (also unaccented) in the 4/4 measures, you would not perceive any change in meter or tempo. However, the accents are what allow the change to be perceived. Included in the concept of "accents" are what other instruments play. In the previous example, the bass line sounded one note on each pulse, where one beat included three eighth notes. In the 4/4 measures, the bass plays one note for every four subdivided notes (sixteenths).

A drummer has many choices as to how to play through such a change. It usually helps to have one instrument such as hi-hat play the subdivisions in both meters. The following example uses the same music as the previous example, but adds the drumset. The hi-hat plays the eighth-note subdivisions in 6/8 and the sixteenth-note subdivisions in 4/4 while the kick simply plays on the pulse. The snare plays on every other pulse to produce a standard backbeat.

Odd and Changing Meter 5

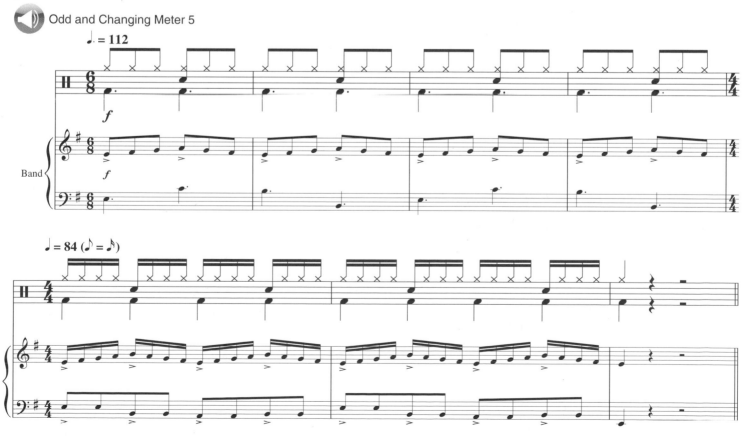

Finally, the next example demonstrates a more elaborate drumset part over the same music. In this case, linear playing has been chosen, where the beat subdivisions are played consistently, but go back and forth between different drums and cymbals.

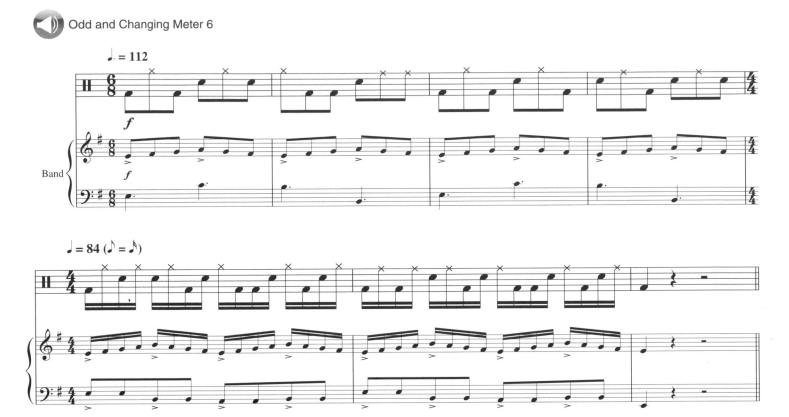

Odd and Changing Meter 6

Hemiola

Like changing meter and odd meter, and metric modulation, *hemiola* is another device that gives the impression of time manipulation. Though the meter may remain constant, a rhythmic pattern consisting of a different length than that of the meter is repeated, thereby beginning on different beats each measure. For example, if the time signature is 4/4, a pattern that is only three beats in length, when repeated without pause, will start on beat four the second time, then beat three the third time, etc. Thus, it begins in different spots "across" the measure, or extends across the barline. If it is repeated enough, it will eventually begin back on beat one again (in this case, the fifth time the pattern is played).

Why not just make the meter 3/4, so the pattern will always begin on beat one, and everything will be neatly in line? Well, this is progressive rock, and having everything neatly in line can be boring; prog players like to shake things up a bit, especially when it comes to issues of time. So even though our pattern is three beats long, other instruments can simultaneously play patterns that are four beats in length. It is the relationship (or conflict) between these patterns of different lengths that makes things interesting. This is a choice that you, the drummer, can make any time you wish to go for an "out-of-sync" feeling and provide for some complexity.

In this next example, the main rhythmic motif is played in the guitar and is four beats long. For the first two measures, the drumset plays a beat that is also four beats, agreeing with the meter and remaining in sync with the guitar riff. In the third measure, the drumset alters its beat to make it only three beats long, thus it starts over again on different beats over measures 3–5. In measure 6, things are back in sync as the beat begins on beat one again. And, in this example, the original beat that was four beats long is played once again in this final measure.

Hemiola 1

If the above example were part of a song your band was composing, you could add to the adventurousness of the section by suggesting the guitar/bass riff be altered by chopping off a beat so it is only three beats long. Then, when the drums play the three-beat pattern, you would all be in sync—at least for a little while. Then, while the guitar and bass continue with the shorter three-beat riff, the drums could play the four-beat pattern, creating a hemiola and reversing the roles of guitar/bass and drumset. This is one way you could get a lot of mileage out of a short riff by manipulating time. And to keep it from getting too monotonous, when the guitar/bass riff gets shortened to three beats, they could transpose it, playing it up a fourth. This might help give the phrases or section a feeling of growth and development.

If you, as the drummer, get inspired to include the hemiola effect, feel free to suggest that another instrument (especially in progressive rock where your band might include a violin, cello, flute, or any instrument outside of the traditional rock band instrumentation) play in sync with you.

The next example employs all of the above suggestions while adding some keyboards into the mix. In the first two measures, guitar, bass, and drums are all in sync in 4/4. Bars 3–5 have the drumset playing a three-beat pattern against the continued four-beat riff to create the hemiola. The left-hand keys enter in bar 3, also playing a pattern three beats long, in sync with the drumset. Measure 6 sees all instruments playing in sync for one bar of 4/4. In measures 7–9, the guitar/bass riff is shortened to three beats while the drumset plays the four-beat pattern. The final two bars see all instruments in sync again playing patterns matching the 4/4 meter.

Hemiola 2

Cross-Rhythms

A *cross-rhythm* is a pattern that contradicts a prevailing rhythmic pattern or meter, and is similar to hemiola (or exactly the same, depending on how it is used). If you were to play steady quarter notes on the ride cymbal at a tempo of quarter = 64, nothing out of the ordinary would be perceived. But if these ride cymbal notes were to be played (at quarter = 64) at the same time as the snare and kick were to play a beat at a tempo of quarter = 96, it might sound like there are two different patterns going on at the same time, but at different tempos, and things might start to get interesting.

The next example demonstrates this concept using the same riff from the previous example. However, this time, the drumset plays a cross-rhythm on the Chinese cymbal. At first, time is played on the ride cymbal in steady eighth notes at a tempo of quarter = 96. In the third measure, the China cymbal is substituted for the ride every three eighth notes. This produces a regular pulse on the China that contradicts the quarter-note pulse of the rest of the music, in that a Chinese cymbal hit occurs every dotted-quarter note. (Also note that it seems to agree with the three-beat organ pattern, in that the Chinese cymbal is on the beat every three beats.)

Cross-Rhythms 1

Mathematically, it works out that if you isolated the China cymbal, it would clock in at 64 beats per minute (take the overall pulse of 96 BPM, multiply that by 2 and then divide that number by 3. 96 X 2 = 192. 192 ÷ 3 = 64). You don't need to do the math to figure out how to employ cross-rhythms. These can be achieved by combining odd numbers with even numbers. For example, if sixteenth notes were played on snare drum (in 4/4), in place of every fifth sixteenth note, play a tom-tom. Because the tom notes are occurring regularly—every five sixteenth notes—the tom hits will have their own steady pulse, which will contradict the quarter-note pulse of the 4/4 meter and whatever beat or pattern the other components of the kit are playing.

Cross-rhythms are prevalent in many different types of music and can be utilized on any instrument. What makes this particular type of cross-rhythm usage special is that it is not simply part of a short riff or motif; rather, the cross-rhythm gets used over an extended period of time, giving the impression of two different pulses or tempos happening simultaneously. And it takes at least a few bars for a particular cross-rhythm to have this effect.

Simple cross-rhythms can be effective when playing in odd meters. The following example shows the cross-rhythm effect occurring every measure. In 7/8, the snare and kick play the same beat every measure, but the ride cymbal changes in its rhythmic placement every bar. Because the ride plays steady quarter notes, the 7/8 meter causes the last ride note to extend over the barline to begin on the second eighth note of the measure. So, every other measure, the ride plays in between the snare/kick rhythm. (Note that, because the ride is independent from the snare and kick, it is notated as its own voice with stems up, with the kick/snare notated as stems down. The nature of this beat requires the need to break from the standard notation of putting notes in the hands in the upstem voice and the feet in a downstem voice.)

Cross-Rhythms 3

Repetition and Variation

This category covers a wide territory, and so only a couple of examples will be used here to demonstrate the concept in a simple way. The drumset parts in the Songs chapter will provide a more thorough demonstration.

All music relies to a degree on some type of repetition. A drummer can take one beat or an element of a particular beat and repeat it, but with something changed. One can simply change a small component of a beat to something different so that it resembles a beat from earlier in the tune. Variation on any element can take place within the same bar, in the following bar, the following phrase, in a later section of the tune, or all of the above. A drummer can also be clever in what gets varied, as well as why and how it does, so to help give deeper meaning to a drumset part and a song as a whole. Deeper levels of repetition and variation are a characteristic of art, and progressive rock is often thought of as an artistic form of rock music.

Reverse Snare/Kick

This technique is often stated in the snare drum with a relationship to the kick, but can be utilized with any drumset component. Since a snare drum hit is such a strong statement within many rock beats, the following technique, when applied to this drum, stands out. Basically, if one takes a simple rock beat in which the snare drum plays the backbeat on beats two and four (in 4/4 time), the drummer may reverse this every other bar, group of bars, or phrase. It is most noticeable when the alternation is at a fairly short time interval, such as every other bar.

The following example illustrates this concept, with the snare switching its rhythmic placement every other measure. Bars 1–4 show this more simply in only the snare while the kick plays "four on the floor." Measures 5–8 keep the snare the same as the first four bars, but now the kick also sees a change in its rhythmic placement every other measure so that the snare and kick fill in each other's gaps. Also note that this kind of rhythmic shifting would not have as much meaning if one were to hear it in the drumset only. If other instruments were to play a riff that was rhythmically the same every measure, the drumset would stand out much more, as it would seem to go in and out of sync with the riff every other measure. The example lets you hear the displacement first without the piano, and then with the riff in order for you to compare the effect.

Reverse Snare/Kick 1

The next example shows a faster metal/punk beat in the context of prog metal. We have a four-bar phrase punctuated by a one-bar unison run, followed by the same four-bar phrase. In the first phrase, the snare is on every "and" of the beat, while the second phrase sees the snare hit on each beat. What emphasizes the effect is that the rest of the band plays the same pattern in both phrases while the drumset alone changes every other one.

Reverse Snare/Kick 2

Rhythmic Unisons

When either the full band or any one instrument plays a riff or melody characterized by a distinctive rhythm, instead of playing a groove underneath it, the progressive drummer may play either the exact same rhythm as the rest of the band, or something close to it. We saw an example of this in the fourth and eighth bars of the previous example.

The next example demonstrates two types of rhythmic unisons within the context of beats. The main rhythmic motif is sounded in the guitar, starting in the first measure, and is four bars in length. The drumset plays a basic rock beat for these first four bars, but in measure 5 plays this rhythm on the snare drum. Punctuating the rhythm guitar parts with snare drum in this fashion is common in metal and prog metal as well as other progressive rock styles. In measure 9, the guitar and keys play the same four-bar rhythm, but this time as a melodic line. The drumset returns to the rock beat for these four bars, but then in measure 13, plays the rhythm around the kit to help add complexity to the guitar/keys line and the rhythmic motif in general.

Rhythmic Unisons

Other Techniques

The following provides brief descriptions of just a few of the many additional techniques that can make for welcome additions to a progressive rock drummer's arsenal.

Double Kick

Persistent double kick with creative parts being played in the hands (something other than a hi-hat or ride keeping time while the snare drum hits backbeats) is common and pretty much a requirement of progressive metal.

Complex rhythms played on the kick drums while the hands play something less complex (e.g., steady timekeeping) can also produce a pattern with some complexity without getting out of control on the technical demands of the drummer. With years of practice, playing fast, complex rhythms on the double kick is not much different than doing so in the hands.

The following are a few basic tips regarding the creation and use of double kick parts. Several of the Drumset Interpretations in the Songs chapter explore double-kick playing. You are also encouraged to explore one of the many double-kick instruction books and videos as well as study with a teacher possessing a high degree of double-kick technique.

- If the rhythm guitar is playing complex rhythms, the kick drums could play the same rhythm.

- If rhythm guitar is playing steady eighths or sixteenths, the drummer should understand that the guitar (and bass) are driving the pulse and that a complex syncopated double kick beat won't get in the way of the groove. It may even help the simpler, steady guitar rhythms seem more adventurous and creative.

- There may be a spot in a tune where guitar and bass completely drop out, and all that is playing are the keys, sounding some atmospheric chords while the vocalist sings. Such a situation may also be a good place for the drummer to be adventurous on the double kicks.

- There is a lot of overlap between progressive metal and other types of metal such as thrash, death, black, power, and many more. In some of these metal styles, what characterizes the drumming is heavy use of the double kick drum. Since progressive rock tends to borrow elements from other styles, what might separate prog metal drumming in any particular song from the drumming in a thrash metal song is simply utilizing metal drumming techniques in smaller doses. After a couple phrases of bombastic double kick beats, the drummer may switch (because of what the other instruments are doing) to something very different, such as a bit of jazz-rock fusion playing. However, the prog metal drummer doesn't always have to rely completely on being reactive to what the other instruments are doing. For example, to employ some repetition with variation, after a couple of phrases (phrase group) of heavy riffs (in guitar, keys, and/or bass), the drummer may make use of a relentless double-kick beat. But then, when the phrase group ends and the same phrase begins anew (perhaps with some minor variations), instead of playing the heavy double-kick beat, the drummer may create and play something that does not seem to be very metal at all. The trick would be to create something that still works and still complements the other instruments and voice(s) while providing for an interesting surprise.

- Metal/double kick techniques can be used in other progressive rock styles such as symphonic or avant-garde. The trick here is to use them sparingly, or at least spend time experimenting to find parts that work within the song. Thoughtful creation along with some patience may allow you to create prog metal-type drumset parts throughout an entire song in an avant-garde or symphonic setting. Remember, just because your band may be firmly in the prog metal style doesn't mean you have to think "metal" in everything you do. It is important in progressive rock to attempt to block out any notions of musical styles and simply create something that sounds good.

Whatever you try in the above situations, give it time to sink in by playing your parts in multiple rehearsals on different days (and record your rehearsals to help you evaluate). Your bandmates may at first question your choices, but they may come to love them after they've gotten comfortable playing along.

Hi-Hat Accents

The hi-hat can create strong accents by hitting the cymbals open, then quickly closing them; this much is obvious, and such usage is widespread across many musical styles. Using such a device two or more times per measure for a whole phrase or more can change the meaning of the technique. Instead of just providing accents, it can serve a similar role to that of the snare drum (or any drum). One way to conceive of this is to take any rock beat, and wherever the snare drum might normally be struck, replace it with a hi-hat accent. More adventurous usage of this technique might be to include hi-hat accents on offbeats where such syncopated placements are particularly effective. Watch for the many instances of this technique in the Songs chapter.

Special Instruments

From specialty cymbals to drums to percussion instruments of other cultures, drummers can add to the overall color of their sound by adding a few components beyond a standard drumset. There are far too many to go into in this book, so you are encouraged to attend concerts of world music, search the Internet for videos, and visit your library and check out recordings. Instruments and techniques from around the world may be just what is needed to give you your own unique sound. The drummer in a prog metal band who incorporates a few Latin or African percussion instruments may find him- or herself playing with a very special voice that many will find appealing. You are encouraged to take any of the songs from the next chapter and add such instruments into the given drumset parts. This includes adding new notes to the parts or substituting a notated drum or cymbal note with a different, perhaps exotic, instrument.

Extended Techniques

This area includes playing any components on the drumset in non-traditional ways, with the following serving as just a very small list out of the many possibilities:

- cymbal scrapes (with a coin or triangle beater)
- rim (on any or all of the drums) and stand (cymbal or other) tapping
- bowing (with string instrument bow) cymbals, rims, and stands
- alternate sticks, e.g., multi-rods, brushes, kitchen utensils, fingers
- cymbal and drum muting (fingers hold or press the instrument while the other hand strikes it; pitch-changes result on toms)
- playing kick drum with sticks, fingers, or attaching an object to the beater
- using snare lever to produce notes as the snares engage the drumhead
- vocalizing while playing the drumkit: this might include anything from singing and speaking to simulating percussion sounds
- drum rub (dragging stick or fingers across head to produce a growl)
- hitting or scraping one stick with the other as the stick being scraped has its tip or end in contact with the drum (shaft may also rest on the rim, and movement of either stick can change pitch and timbre)

For more information on these techniques, including audio and video examples, you are encouraged to research and explore.

And remember, if your bandmates (or you) compose and arranged a complete tune, with all of the instrumental and vocal parts in place, and you are asked to create drumset parts, don't let what the other instruments are doing be written in stone. You may come up with something for a particular moment or phrase that you are really proud of, but it doesn't quite gel with the other instruments. However, a few subtle tweeks to the guitar, bass, and/or keys may allow your drumset part to work perfectly.

■ Chapter 3
SONGS: DRUMSET INTERPRETATION AND COMPOSITION

This chapter includes nine short songs that make use of basic progressive techniques as well as individual choices based on the situations created by the other instruments. It presents multiple drumset-part possibilities, labeled as "Interpretations." An effort has been made to create songs that embody the styles of well-known progressive rock bands, with some songs emulating a combination of more than one band. Interpretations may also be based on the drumming styles associated with these bands.

Procedures for Creation

Since this chapter, and the whole book for that matter, is designed to help you create progressive drumset parts, before the songs are presented, this section outlines some general procedures that may be followed in order to create a drumset part. These may be utilized when attempting to create a drumset part for the songs in this chapter as well as any time you're given instrumental music and asked to come up with drumset parts to accompany it. Three possible procedures are presented, with each procedure being made up of several steps. There is no one correct procedure to follow, and you may come up with your own method. Consider these procedures when studying each song in this chapter.

Procedure 1: Listen, Visualize, and Play

A. First, listen to the "minus drums" (or "play-along") track at least three times without playing. Before you allow drumset beats composed by someone else to get inside your head, allow yourself to think creatively first. On the first listen, try not to imagine drumset at all; just absorb the music. Think about rhythmic characteristics: What is distinctive about the rhythms? Does one instrument's rhythmic qualities stand out over another? On the second listen, just think about what the drumset might do. On the third listen, think about the progressive techniques from Chapter Two, what you might use, and then just tap along on your legs or a tabletop. Then, get behind the kit and play along with the track. Don't worry if you don't quite make use of all the creative ideas you imagined on the previous listen. Just try to capture a bit of the feel as you play along. However, it may be risky to simply play along with a standard rock beat, as once you do this (and the more you do it), it can be more difficult to get this sound and feel out of your head. So it is recommended that you first attempt to play along with a very simple yet non-traditional beat. One method is to just play on two drums/cymbals, such as hi-hat and kick drum only.

B. Second, listen to and study the different drumset interpretations provided. Practice them and play along with the audio.

C. Third, attempt to create your own drumset part. This may involve combining elements from the different interpretations in this book into one part. It may also involve a completely new part that only uses a few small bits from the book, but with your own variations as well as completely new elements. You can attempt to create your part by playing along with the track many times. You may need to stop the track and try out a few things slowly to practice your ideas without the distraction of the audio.

Procedure 2: Listen, Read, and Write

A. First, follow Step A from Procedure 1 until you are asked to play. This procedure is designed to get you thinking creatively without letting the mechanical limitations of your limbs get in the way. When listening to the play-along track, simply imagine a drumset part using your "inner ear."

B. Second, listen to and study the different drumset interpretations provided, but do not play them at the kit.

C. Third, after you've imagined what you might create, then listened to and studied the provided interpretations, go back and attempt to create your own drumset part. The difference here (from Procedure 1) is that you are to do so only by listening to the audio and then writing your ideas down, without ever touching the drumkit.

Procedure 3: Listen/Read and Write/Play

This procedure is a combination of Procedures 1 and 2. First, follow the steps for Procedure 2, but then go back and practice the provided interpretations, and then attempt to play what you notated. As you do this, make changes so that you end up combining the best of what you imagined with what worked as you actually tested out your ideas and sculpted new ones at the drumset.

It is recommended that when you attempt to create a drumset part for a song, you try to create two different interpretations. Your first interpretation should simply exist as the best progressive rock drumset music you can come up with (i.e., knowing that you will be attempting to create two drumset parts, don't leave an idea out, saving it for your second interpretation).

After you come up with something you are proud of, attempt to create a second interpretation (you could do this immediately, the next day, or even a week or more later). For the second interpretation, don't simply create a variation of the first or try to improve upon the first. Make every effort to create something as different as you can. This may help you explore options and make choices you normally wouldn't come up with.

When you finish, examine both interpretations, and if you like, create a third that combines the best elements of the first two. You might wish to use this method when creating drumset parts in your band. The end results as well as the procedures can help to expand your creative thinking and increase your drumset chops, taking you to new levels of virtuosity.

Songs and Interpretations

While some drumset techniques and other musical choices will be discussed in the text, only those that may not be immediately obvious will be included. You are encouraged to listen and study the scores and make your own observations, just as you would when listening to your favorite bands. Doing so will help you in your own creative endeavors.

Red Charge

Between the keyboards, guitar, and bass, we sometimes have three very different rhythmic parts going on simultaneously. It may be common to choose a drumset part that closely follows the rhythms of the bass (or bass and guitar, as the two sometimes play the same part, an octave apart). But closely following the rhythm of the main melody, whether stated by an instrument or voice, can produce something interesting. Be careful, as such an avenue runs the risk of the band loosing the feel of a strong pulse. While this might produce something appealing, it can also be more difficult to keep together in a live setting.

INTERPRETATION A

Besides the high energy level of the first drumset part, what makes this a bit tricky to play is the snare drum on the first beat of the measure, beginning with the beat in measure 17. If you're used to playing traditional rock, the urge to play the kick on the first beat of the measure, in any meter, feels natural.

The thirty-second notes in the kick drum from the beginning may not require the use of a double kick. Since they are relegated to groups of two, it may be executed as a double stroke would in the hands, where the second note is just a quick bounce.

Pay attention to how the drumset follows the rhythm of the instruments (or which instruments are followed).

In measures 31–32, a cross-rhythm effect in the guitar/bass makes it sound as if suddenly the quarter note, instead of the dotted quarter, is providing the pulse. This provides for the illusion of a tempo change. This drumset interpretation plays along with the guitar/bass manipulation of time to further the illusion as the China and hi-hat accentuate the bass/guitar rhythm.

"Red Charge," Interpretation A

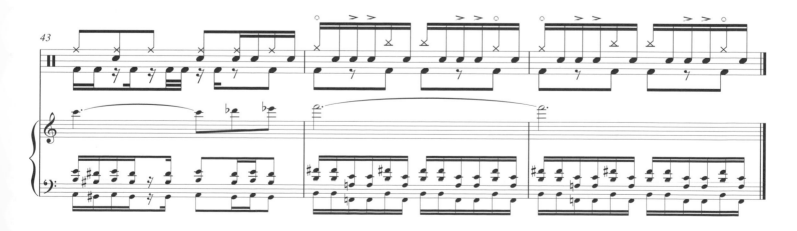

INTERPRETATION B

This interpretation makes more use of the snare playing on beat one, right from the beginning.

Starting in measure 9, where this is a repeat of the music from measures 1–8, the drumset employs some variation. Besides changing from hi-hat to ride (very common in many styles of music), ghost notes in the snare are included, and kick drum notes and rhythms have been slightly changed.

The cross-rhythm effect (mm. 31–32) is still accented in the drumset, but this time by the snare drum within a tom-tom beat.

"Red Charge," Interpretation B

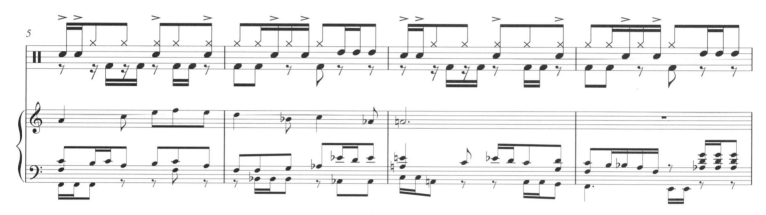

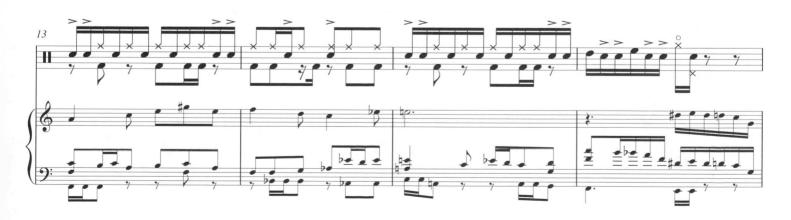

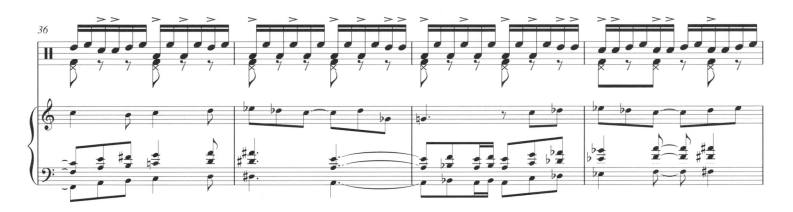

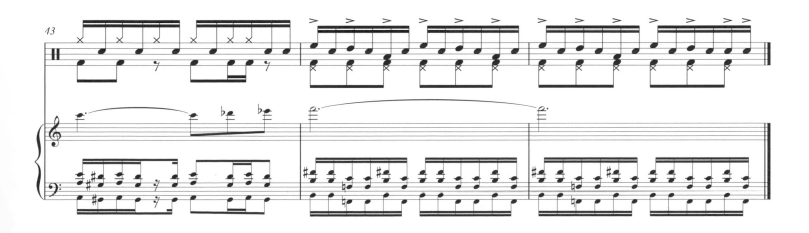

"Red Charge," Play-Along

There is a chart for this song in the Appendix, which has a blank drumset staff on which you can create your own part.

INTERPRETATION C

With a heavy use of the double kick, this part falls in the "progressive metal" category. Effort has been made to resist playing steady sixteenth notes too long, and allow sixteenth-note patterns to be interrupted by the snare drum to form some syncopations.

Beginning in measure 25, a bit of a cross-rhythm pattern is played between the hi-hat and splash. Because they alternate every eighth note, the hi-hat plays on the first and third eighth notes of the first dotted-quarter note beat, but on the second half of the measure, this gets reversed.

The previously mentioned cross-rhythm effect from measure 31 gets treated as more of a fill in this interpretation. If you were to isolate the drumset (try playing these two bars on your own, at any tempo), it sounds as if it were a fill in simple rather than compound meter. It may most resemble a bar of 4/4 followed by a bar of 2/4. These measures can be tricky to play because of this cymbal pattern. Practice this first by playing just the hi-hat on each eighth-note beat (replacing the alternating splash and occasional crash once you can execute the rest of the beat confidently).

"Red Charge," Interpretation C

(Bonus interpretation, no audio provided)

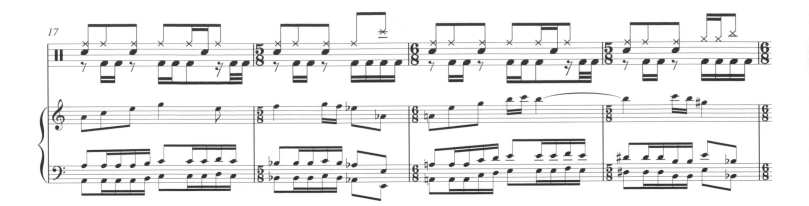

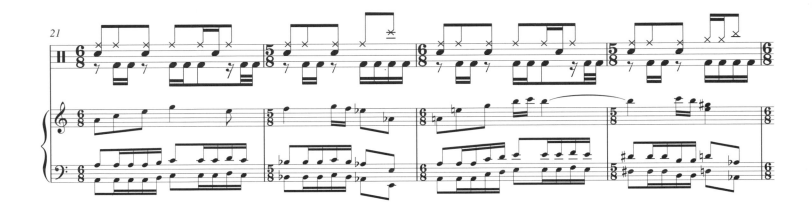

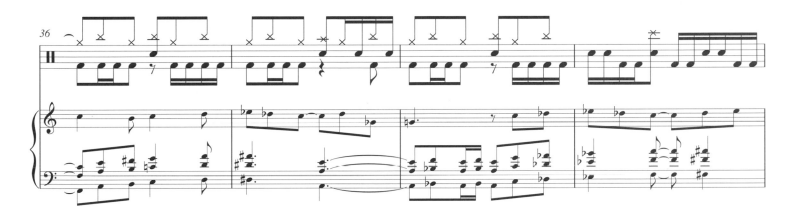

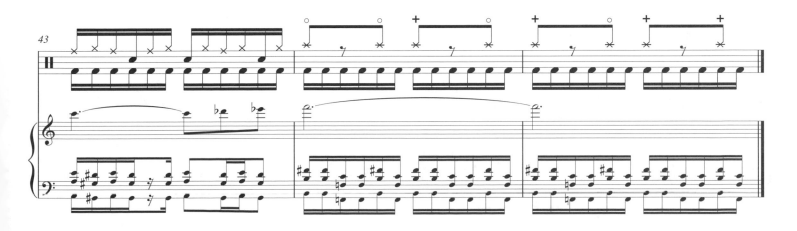

Quintuple Bypass

This short tune is designed to get you used to playing in 5/8 but is otherwise straightforward.

INTERPRETATION A

The first interpretation is fairly obvious in its use of techniques. A linear drumbeat undergoes variation in measure 9 when the China cymbal replaces the hi-hat. Also, to help give the tune more drive in its second half, measures 9, 11, 13, and 15 see an additional kick drum note (compared to measures 1–8), providing for kick drum sixteenths in every bar from 9 to the end. One reason to provide variation, and this type of variation, is in a final section of a tune in order to give the ending something special, perhaps signaling finality.

"Quintuple Bypass," Interpretation A

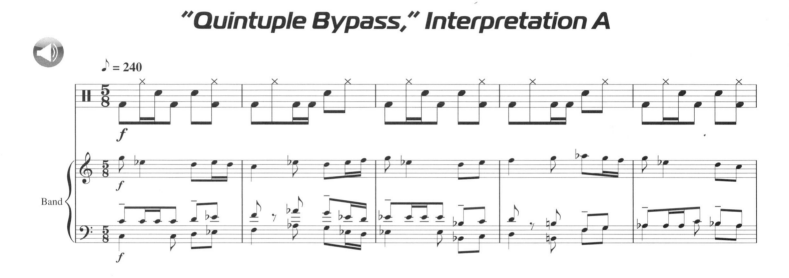

INTERPRETATION B

The open/closed hi-hat on the second eighth-note beat provides a strong accent to emphasize the syncopation in the keyboard melody. This helps highlight the asymmetry of the meter, where the 5/8 is felt as a 3+2 subdivision, and so the hi-hat accent goes against where the big beats of the measure lie (on 1 and 4). Such rhythmic conflict can provide an extra layer of complexity.

"Quintuple Bypass," Interpretation B

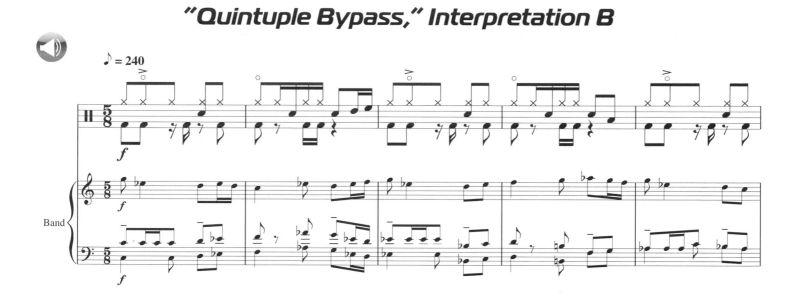

"Quintuple Bypass," Play-Along

There is a chart for this song in the Appendix, which has a blank drumset staff on which you can create your own part.

INTERPRETATION C

The overt double kick makes this a prog metal interpretation. In measure 9, where ride takes over for hi-hat once again, a China cymbal is sounded every two eighth notes. This produces a cross-rhythm effect in that the first measure has the China cymbal on 2 and 4, and the second bar has it on 1, 3, and 5.

"Quintuple Bypass," Interpretation C

(Bonus interpretation, no audio provided)

The Cool Northern Sun

The first of the two main sections of this song is dominated by the bass, playing in a soloistic fashion. In measure 24, the song switches gears a bit with keyboard and guitar taking over in the foreground.

INTERPRETATION A

The drumset part follows the bass rhythms closely in this first interpretation, to the point that from measures 1 through 16, there is little overt repetition. This produces almost a kind of drum solo rather than a beat. When an instrumental part plays in such a soloistic fashion, if the part is composed (as opposed to improvised), the drummer can create something elaborate if it is closely connected to the rhythmic characteristics of the solo part. Such elaboration won't get in the way of the soloistic part, whereas a busy groove might. If a solo is improvised, the drummer should get out of the way at least a bit more, where the desire is usually to be complex rather than complicated (or confusing).

In measure 24, when the band is grooving along at a steady pulse, we see an enhanced version of a typical rock 'n' roll drumbeat. The "four on the floor" kick drum is very simple in establishing the pulse, while the rhythms in the hands, especially the placement of the snare and tom notes, help accent the syncopated character of the other instruments. This concept can be applied to any drumbeats you create. Instead of a backbeat snare on 2 and 4, put the snare on the "and" of the beat.

"The Cool Northern Sun," Interpretation A

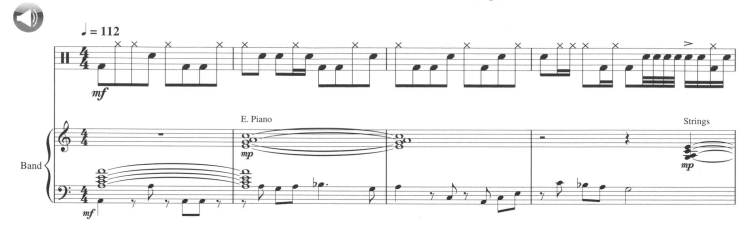

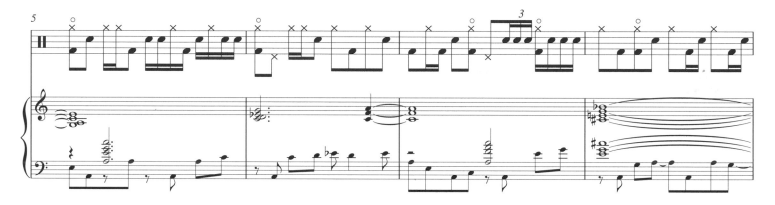

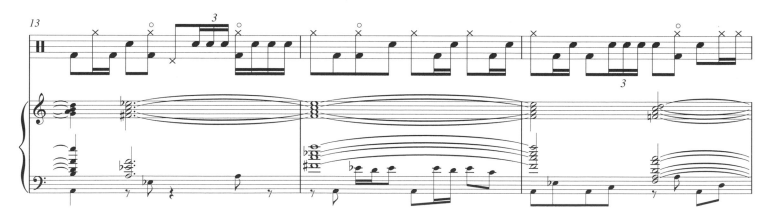

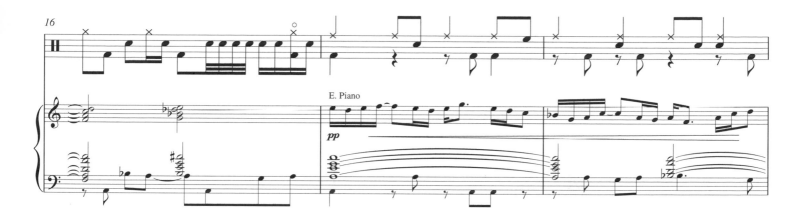

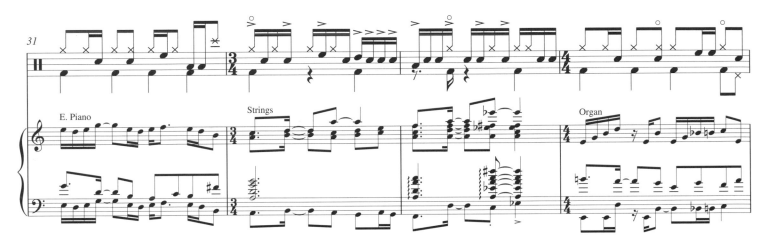

INTERPRETATION B

While Interpretation A has the drumset playing something different every bar to accompany the soloistic bass part in the first section, Interpretation B sets more of a steady groove in four-bar phrases. This can make it easier for the bass player, giving him something grounded, especially if the bass part involves an element of improvisation. The drumbeat still plays a rhythm that characterizes the bass part, overall (the bass rhythm as in measure 1 is used throughout the first section, even though the pitches played make for a bass part with not a lot of repetition).

In measure 17, the basic beat continues, but with the China cymbal playing on beats 2 and 4, a variation employed to coincide with the entrance of the electric piano part.

To further draw attention to the fact that a new section of music begins in measure 24, the drumset launches into a double-time beat every other bar (measures 24, 26, 28, 30, and 34). There is also some variation in these measures in the form of a switch in the rhythmic placement of the kick and snare. For example, when comparing measure 24 with 26, you will see that the kick and snare have changed places.

In measures 25, 27, 29, 31, and 35, the cross-rhythms in the keyboards/guitar/bass are emphasized in the drumset. There is a rhythmic pattern, six sixteenth notes in length that repeats, producing the illusion of a change in tempo, and a feeling of a shuffle pattern (for at least the first three beats, it feels like the meter is 6/16, with a dotted-eighth pulse).

"The Cool Northern Sun," Interpretation B

*The audio features two sixteenth-note pickups to the beginning of the tune.

48

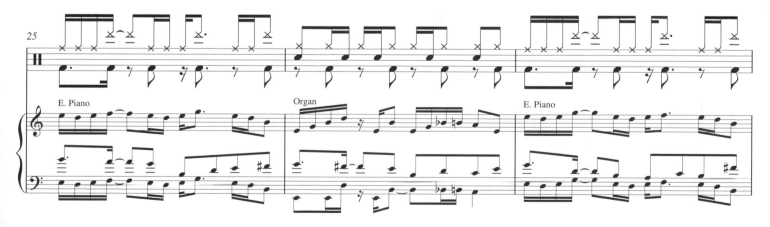

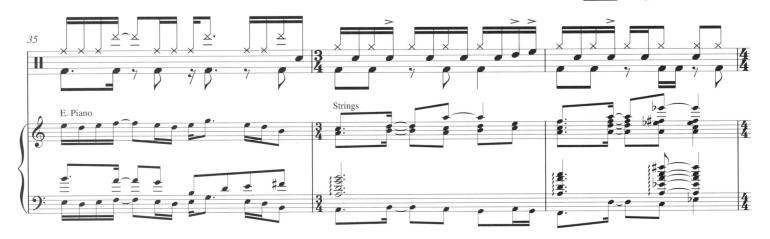

"The Cool Northern Sun," Play-Along

There is a chart for this song in the Appendix, which has a blank drumset staff on which you can create your own part.

Am I Awake?

Being one of the longer tunes in the book, this song is divided into three main sections, with the final section a repeat of the first. The middle section (measures 18–49) are characterized by a very different mood, with softer dynamics, and a 7/8 meter. This odd meter may be subdivided as 2+2+3.

INTERPRETATION A

In the second section (m. 18), the drums switch from a busy, driving rock beat to a simple, linear beat played softly. Progressive rock is often defined by change and contrast, and even the heaviest bands aren't afraid to create something more delicate in nature. Playing a linear beat in such sections can allow the drummer to play quietly without sounding too busy, yet still avoid sounding like traditional rock 'n' roll.

As this section progresses, the drumset makes changes in several stages. Measure 26 sees the drumset part changing quite a bit, helping these different stages build in dynamics and intensity. Also, even though the 7/8 pattern is consistently defined by a 2+2+3 subdivision, the drumset does not accent these subdivisions the same way every measure. Notice how in measure 26, the kick and snare play the same rhythm as the bass, yet in the following measure, even though the bass restates the same rhythm, the drumset plays "in between the cracks" of the bass part. Any time an instrument plays a repeated rhythmic pattern, the drummer can avoid predictability by emulating this rhythm only every other time the pattern is sounded. This might help the rhythmic feel produce a stronger sense of growth and forward motion.

"Am I Awake?," Interpretation A

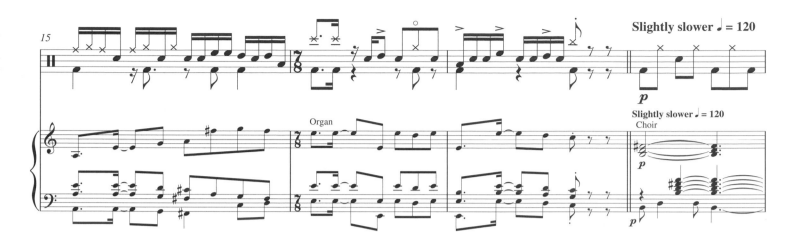

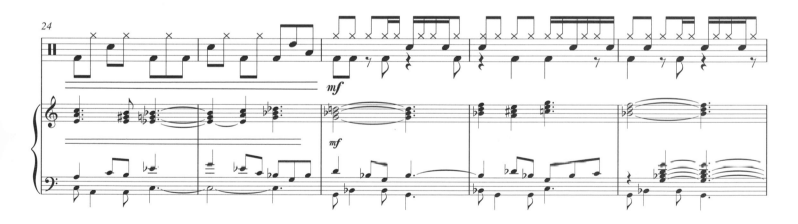

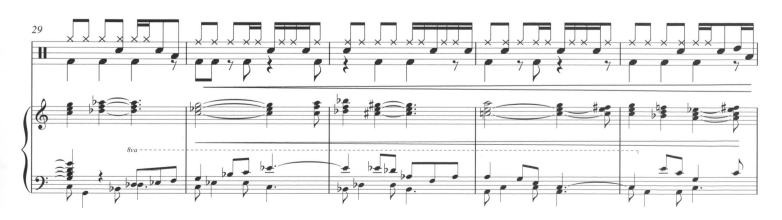

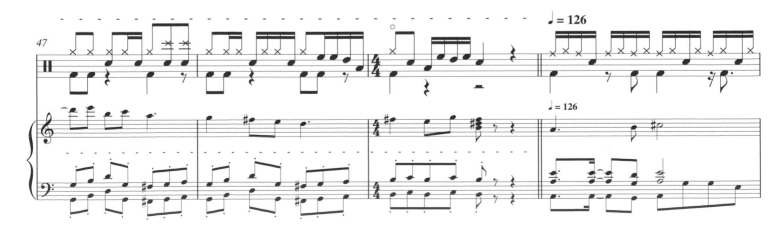

INTERPRETATION B

In contrast to the drumset part in Interpretation A, Interpretation B starts out with a beat that plays the snare on beat one. The rhythms of this beat more strongly mimic the rhythms in the guitar and bass parts in these opening bars.

Beginning in measure 6, the drumset manipulates time a bit by playing a more rhythmically spacious beat. There is a rhythmic pattern six eighth notes in length that repeats, creating the feeling that the drumset is in 6/8 while the rest of the band is in 4/4. This will become more apparent if you play these bars on the drumset alone, without the rest of the band. However, this isn't done simply to create the complex sounding hemiola; rather, the rhythmic pattern works with the rhythms sounded in the lead guitar.

In the 7/8 section, beginning in measure 38, the stack cymbal starts on the second eighth-note beat, playing every two beats. This produces a cross-rhythm effect in that the first bar sees the stack on the even beats, alternating every other measure where the stack is placed on the odd beats.

"Am I Awake?," Interpretation B

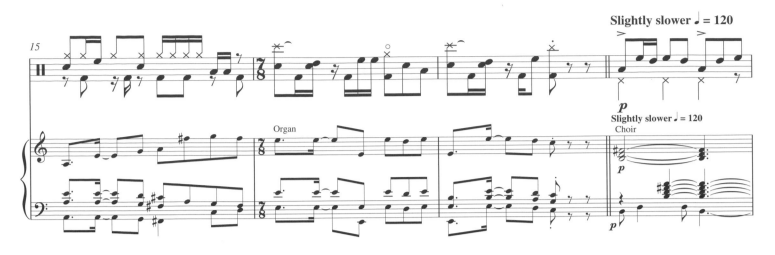

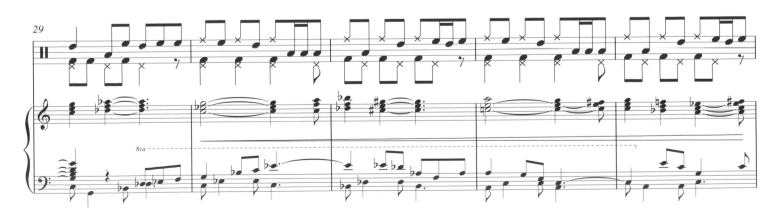

Displacement in stack: playing
every other eighth note means
the cymbal is on the different side
of the beat every other measure.

59

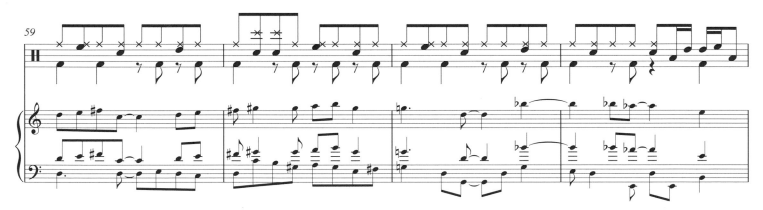

"Am I Awake?" Play-Along

There is a chart for this song in the Appendix, which has a blank drumset staff on which you can create your own part.

INTERPRETATION C

This is another interpretation in the kick drum-heavy progressive metal style.

"Am I Awake?," Interpretation C

(Bonus interpretation, no audio provided)

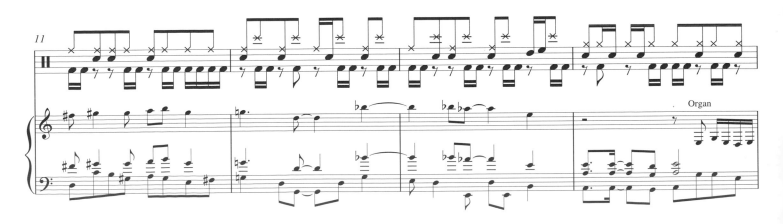

Slightly slower ♩ = 120

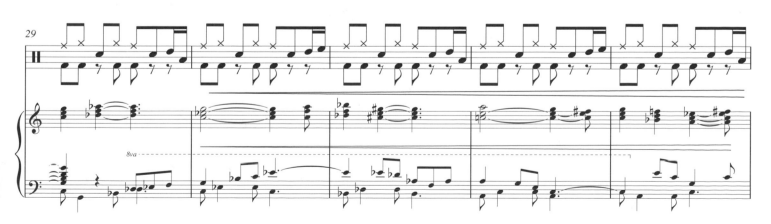

63

Mind Control

This song has two main sections, with the second half of the tune being a heavier repeat of the first.

INTERPRETATION A

The drumset part in this interpretation is characterized by quick linear patterns in the hands between the hi-hat and snare. Rather than have consistent eighths keep time in the hi-hat, the sixteenths played in linear fashion with the snare provide some added interest.

Beginning in measure 11, the pattern switches to the ride cymbal and then an offbeat stack cymbal in measure 15.

Repeating a section of music, rather than playing a consistent variation for the whole repeat, can help provide drive to change things up more often. Simply playing a different beat for an entire repeated section can be a bit predictable itself.

"Mind Control," Interpretation A

INTERPRETATION B

The double kick in this interpretation is so "in your face" it is almost comical, especially in the first half of the tune where the band is not playing particularly heavy. However, such over-the-top playing, whether the tune is humorous or ironic in any way or not, can make for entertaining music. A drummer should consider this tactic in smaller doses (one or two tunes on an album at most) to be effective without sounding like a parody.

A cross-rhythm ride (played on the dome or bell) such as that seen in measures 11–16 can make for an effective rhythm in 6/8 (the ride plays every two eighth notes, which makes it sound like a simple meter such as 4/4).

"Mind Control," Interpretation B

"Mind Control," Play-Along

There is a chart for this song in the Appendix, which has a blank drumset staff on which you can create your own part.

Mad Science

This song features a fairly simple syncopated riff and straightforward repetition. Such music can be a good place for the drummer to really groove. This is another three-part song where the first and third parts are the same basic material. A short *coda* (an ending phrase or section meant to give a tune finality, here stated in measures 29–31) can be a good place for a drummer to flourish.

INTERPRETATION A

Steady quarters on the stack cymbal are prevented from sounding too dull because of the syncopations in the snare, kick, and toms. When playing a beat where the snare is not relegated to playing the backbeat (or on the beat at all), but plays often in between the beat, keeping time on a cymbal in a simple and steady fashion can help the syncopated drums stand out.

Starting in measure 11, where the music changes a bit, a heavily accented syncopation in the open-then-closed hi-hat keeps things from sounding too square.

At measure 18 when the first beat returns, the only change is that instead of the stack cymbal, a China cymbal is called for. This is just a minor change in orchestration to provide subtle variation to the repetition. Also, the China cymbal, with its longer decay, may be perceived as a bit more grand, suitable for an ending.

"Mad Science," Interpretation A

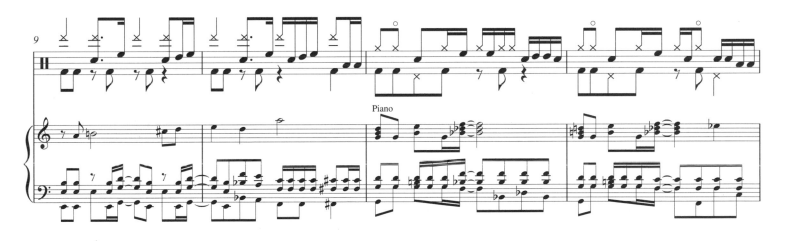

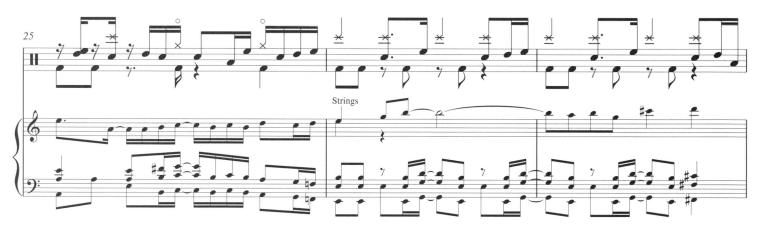

INTERPRETATION B

The second interpretation starts out with a hi-hat accent on the "and" of beat 1, similar to what was played in the middle section of Interpretation A. This first beat also makes use of sixteenth-note linear patterns in the hands.

The start of the middle section at measure 11 is primarily just a slight variation on the first beat, with ride replacing hi-hat.

"Mad Science," Interpretation B

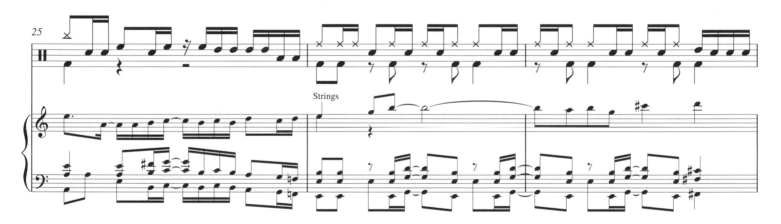

"Mad Science," Play-Along

There is a chart for this song in the Appendix, which has a blank drumset staff on which you can create your own part.

Below Zero

Another syncopated riff in the guitar/bass drives this tune. A short bass solo in measures 10–12 provide for an important contrast a drummer must carefully consider.

The 7/8 bars starting in measure 15 feature the same basic music as in the beginning, but with an eighth-note beat chopped off to provide for a bit of asymmetrical interest.

INTERPRETATION A

This drumset part makes a concentrated use of many of the techniques from Chapter 2 in a short span of time. Looking at the first two bars alone, you may notice the use of syncopated open-then-closed hi-hat, tom-tom beats, double kick, and offbeat China/stack.

The double kick drum in measure 2 may be seen as foreshadowing the staccato sixteenths in the guitar part in measure 4. These eight sixteenth notes may be seen as a primary motif of this song, and as such, the motif occurs at the very end of the tune. The motif does not occur in the guitar until measure 4, and then it is only sounded in the form of four (instead of eight) staccato sixteenths in measures 11, 12, and 21. And so it is the drumset that more firmly establishes this as a motif by foreshadowing it and repeating it more often. This demonstrates one way the drummer can provide for an important element to the compositional structure of a tune. If you, as the drummer, were given this keyboards/guitar/bass music and were asked to create a drumset part, the staccato sixteenths may have caught your ear. And because this occurred, even though these guitar notes did not dominate the tune, you decided to turn it into something bigger.

Bass solos can be tricky with respect to orchestration. In the studio, one can easily mix such a solo to make sure it is heard no matter what else is going on. However, in a live setting, what accompanies a bass solo can be very important. In the case of this interpretation, linear playing and avoidance of crash cymbals can allow the drummer to play something interesting while allowing the bass solo to stand out in the mix.

The 7/8 bar (measure 15) takes the same beat as measure 14 and just splices out the first hi-hat/kick note sounded on beat 3, jumping right into the open-then-closed hi-hat note.

"Below Zero," Interpretation A

INTERPRETATION B

This tom-tom beat-dominated drumset part with the snares turned off makes for a considerable contrast to Interpretation A. The kick and hi-hat-with-foot statements help bring about the rhythms in the guitar/bass. Whereas the snare is struck on beat 3 in measure 1, in the second bar the snare is played on the "and" of 1 to avoid predictability, even though the tom-tom beat is very similar.

For the bass solo in measure 10, the drumset gets even more out of the way (compared with Interpretation A) by playing mostly hi-hat and kick with sparse snare drum. Also note that having the snares turned off produces a timbre that has less chance of drowning out a bass solo.

Measure 13, which sees the guitar and bass drop out while the keyboards take over with a high-register run, exhibits something different from Interpretation A. Instead of dropping out with the rest of the band, the drumset plays as pseudo-unison rhythm with the piano. Fast runs, whether characterized by steady sixteenths or broken up by some syncopations, can provide an opportunity for the drummer also to show off a bit with a fill that is tightly locked into the instrumental run. Just like the bass part in "The Cool Northern Sun," such a situation is reliant on whether the instrumental part is composed, improvised, or a combination of the two.

"Below Zero," Interpretation B

"Below Zero," Play-Along

There is a chart for this song in the Appendix, which has a blank drumset staff on which you can create your own part.

Sky Blade

Along with "Am I Awake?" this song is the most complete in the book. "Sky Blade" is made up of two large sections that may be broken up into six subsections, as follows:

- **A**: mm. 1–16
  - ➤ a: 1–8
  - ➤ b: 9–16
- **B**: mm. 17–48
  - ➤ a: 17–30
  - ➤ b: 31–38
  - ➤ c: 39–43
  - ➤ d: 44–48

With each new subsection, the dynamic and energy levels rise a bit. A drummer should consider this to help bring out these changes and the overall build. Gradually playing louder with each new subsection may be effective, but would only provide for an obvious complement to the dynamic structure.

INTERPRETATION A

Due to the heavily syncopated guitar and piano parts at the beginning, the drumset could either lay way back and play it simple, or tackle the challenge of creating something just as complex that doesn't clutter up this overall tranquil section. This interpretation attempts the latter, accenting the syncopations with the snare and kick while the hi-hat fills in almost every sixteenth-note subdivision. This role of the hi-hat is done to help promote a steady flow so that the syncopations are not perceived as jarring interruptions. Only part of a backbeat snare is used, where it is accented on beat 4.

In measure 9, the addition of the ride to form a ride/hi-hat combination increases the dynamics due to the sustaining effect of the ride cymbal.

In measure 17, the song makes a big shift from tranquil acoustic-driven rock to heavy rock. To provide for cohesion, the drumset in measure 21 plays a similar ride-hi-hat combination to measure 9, but with the dynamic level up to *forte*. Because the drummer knows what is coming up later, he or she can wait on bringing in a new, heavier beat at this point, even though the guitar has entered the land of metal. This might help the tune continue to build without giving away too much too soon. This concept is applied to the rest of the song, with some of the heaviest drum statements occurring in measures 31–34, and especially measures 39–42 where the drumset is the most driven, playing in a double-time feel.

Measures 44 to the end may be seen as a coda, worthy of something different that has not been heard elsewhere in the song. Thus, a tom-tom beat with driving, steady eighths in the kick/hi-hat w/foot provide for a grand finale.

"Sky Blade," Interpretation A

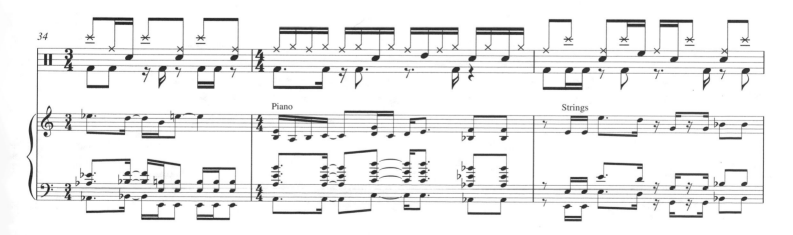

INTERPRETATION B

A bit of extra compositional strategy went into the drumset part for the first 16 bars of Interpretation B. This is basically a two-bar pattern that gets repeated under some variation in bars 3 and 4, forming a four-bar pattern. The kick drum is the same in every measure. The hands in measure 2 play nearly the same thing as measure 1, except for the last beat. Now, measure 3 is similar to measure 1, except the hi-hat notes and tom-tom notes switch positions (first, the hi-hat plays on the "and" of 1 and the tom on the "a" of 2, but in measure 3, these get switched). Also compare measure 2 with measure 4. On the last beat of measure 2, the floor tom is played on the first two sixteenths, followed by a China cymbal hit on the "and" of the beat. In measure 4, the China cymbal comes first, on the beat, followed by the floor tom.

To the casual listener, this may sound like two bars that repeat, but subconsciously, one might perceive the variation. Subtlety is an important part of art, and this type of variation, although simple, can provide for some artistic subtlety that attaches itself into deeper layers of the listener. This type of variation can come out of just playing as you create a drum part, but it is much easier (and faster) to think for a minute, plan this out, and then play/write it.

In measure 17, a tom tom beat, colored by a grace note on the snare that ornaments the tom hit, is closely connected to the rhythm of the guitar. The "four-on-the-floor" kick helps anchor the syncopations in the toms.

The beat in measure 25 is echoed in measure 26, but in the latter bar, the snare and kick drum trade places in their rhythmic placements. When this two-bar beat returns in measure 29, instead of the strong China cymbal hit on beat one, it is delayed until beat 2. Cymbal crashes on the downbeat are all too common. There is nothing wrong with making such a statement, but after it is done once, when a similar phrase returns, it may be effective to delay the cymbal hit a bit. The listener will be expecting it on beat 1, and when it doesn't happen until half a beat or a beat later, it can have even more impact than the first hit. When employing such a strategy, see if one of the other instrumentalists can join you with a keyboard stab, guitar gliss, or something to add to your statement as you delay this hit.

The coda (measure 43) again sees something different than what was played in the rest of the tune (as well as something quite different from Interpretation A). Where the guitar and bass play constant sixteenth notes that are not accented (although slurred or "hammered" notes on a guitar might produce slight accents, as this technique involves picking only the first note in the slur and the following notes are sounded with the left hand only as they are fingered on the fretboard), the drumset plays a sixteenth-note pattern with strong, syncopated accents. The accents that result are sounded in the open-then-closed hi-hat and China/stack cymbal hits— even though some snare drum notes are marked with an accent (this has more to do with indicated ghost notes rather than strongly accented snare drum hits).

"Sky Blade," Interpretation B

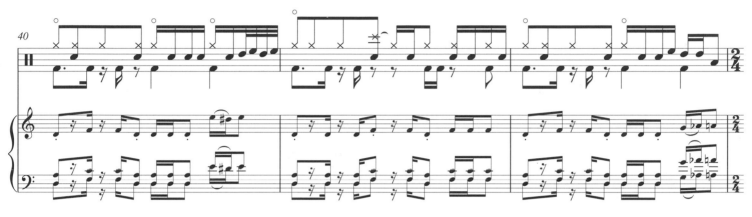

"Sky Blade," Play-Along

There is a chart for this song in the Appendix, which has a blank drumset staff on which you can create your own part.

Cyborg Sleeper

This entire song is in 7/8, but it is a different type of 7/8 than we've seen before. Where this meter is often subdivided as either 2+2+3 or 3+2+2, this song uses both. The meters are grouped in twos where the first bar is 2+2+3 and the second is 3+2+2, and it follows this pattern consistently throughout the song. The main theme of the tune, sounded in the keyboards in measures 1–4, is a palindrome rhythm (which is an obvious choice due to the fact that the combination of these two 7/8 measures, which are subdivided differently from each other, also form a palindrome).

A quieter middle section that builds up to a louder dynamic (measures 27–60) provides the drummer with the challenge of creating interesting beats that serve the mood of the tune.

INTERPRETATION A

This drumset part is characterized by quick little linear patterns in the hands between the snare and either hi-hat or ride, as is seen throughout measures 1–36.

Navigating the palindrome rhythm and meter is made easier once you listen to the tune and get the keyboard melody in your head. It also helps to count out loud as you listen.

When the dynamic level drops in measure 37, we again see the use of a simpler linear beat to help reflect the new mood. Offbeat China cymbal hits in measures 49–52 help enhance the dynamic build before the energy level ramps up in measure 53. At this spot, open-then-closed hi-hat stabs help accent the subdivisions in the pulse, making the palindrome stand out even more than before.

Measures 61 to the end are a return to the first section of the song, and so the drumming repeats as well.

"Cyborg Sleeper," Interpretation A

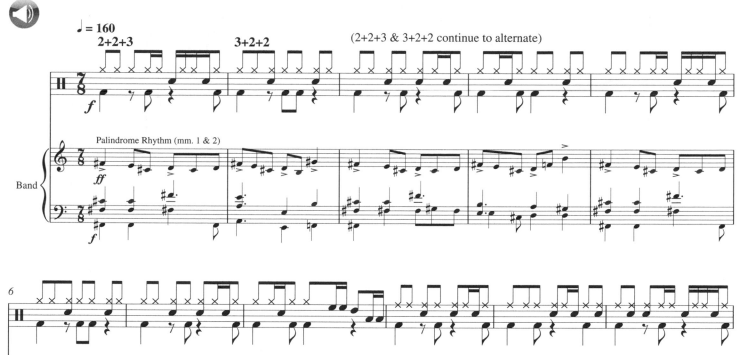

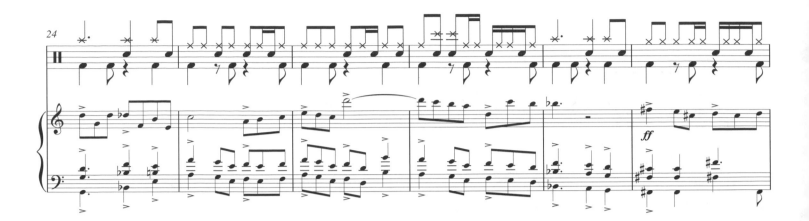

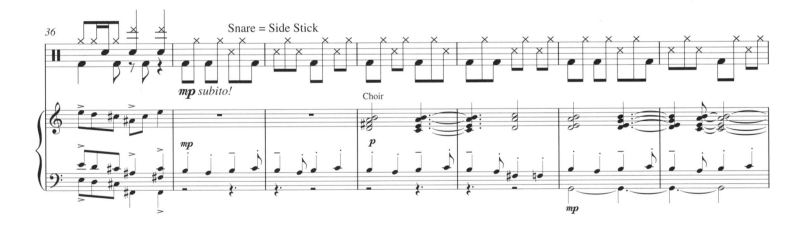

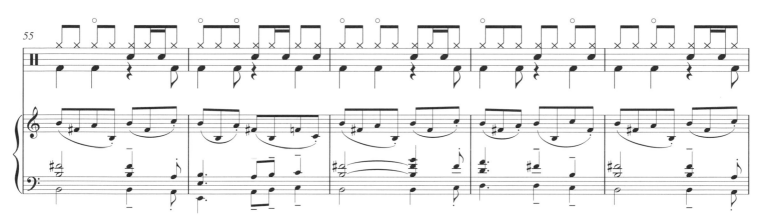

INTERPRETATION B

Hi-hat stabs are used in this interpretation as well, but right from the beginning. However, instead of going for the more predictable choice of accenting beat 1 with the hi-hat, this pattern waits until beat 2.

To provide a contrast with Interpretation A, the middle section of this version makes use of a tom-tom beat (measure 37). The kick and ride interrupt the tom-toms in order to accent notes in the bass.

Another contrast to Interpretation A is that in measures 56–60, a linear beat characterizes the end to this middle section where the music has risen in dynamics and energy. In Interpretation A, linear playing was used at the much quieter start of the middle section. This demonstrates that a linear beat can be used in both types of mood and dynamics.

In measure 61 to the end, rather than repeat the same drumset part from the beginning, this interpretation employs some variation with the addition of the China cymbal. To further the challenge of the two-7/8-bar palindrome that characterizes this song, the China begins on the third eighth-note beat and then plays steady quarters. This allows the China to be struck at different places in each bar for four bars until it returns to being struck on the third eighth-note beat in measure 65. This is just one final example demonstrating how a cross-rhythm, especially in 7/8, can produce the illusion that the China cymbal is playing in a different meter from the rest of the drumset (and the rest of the band).

"Cyborg Sleeper," Interpretation B

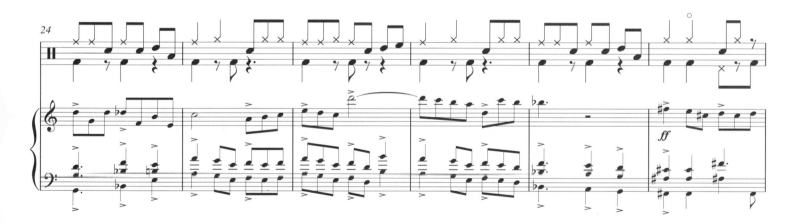

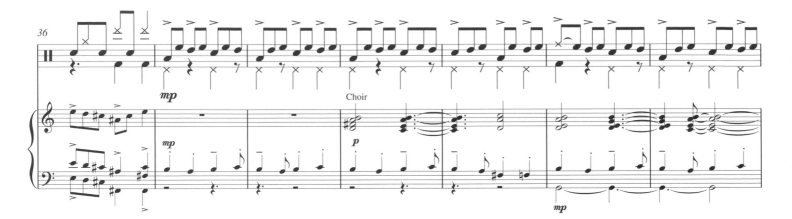

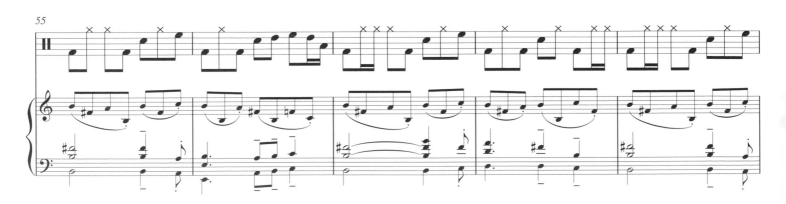

"Cyborg Sleeper," Play-Along

There is a chart for this song in the Appendix, which has a blank drumset staff on which you can create your own part.

■ *Appendix*

BAND SCORES WITH BLANK DRUMSET STAVES

Use the scores in the Appendix to notate the drumset parts you create. If you have access to recording technology, record your drumset parts as you perform with the play-along tracks.

Red Charge

 "Red Charge," Play-Along

$\bullet = 84$

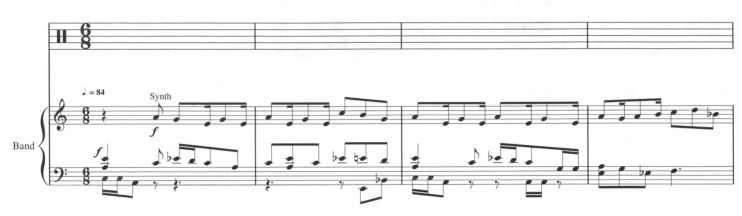

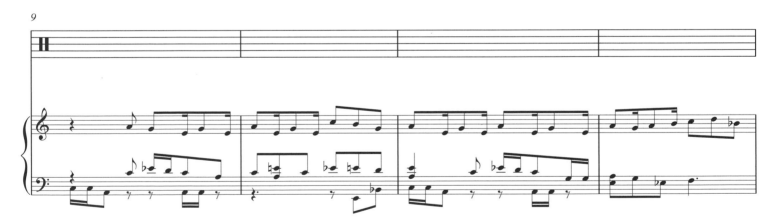

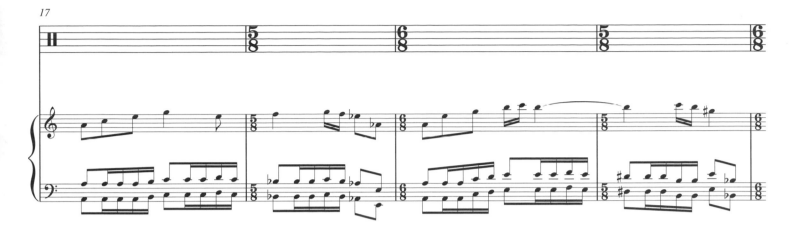

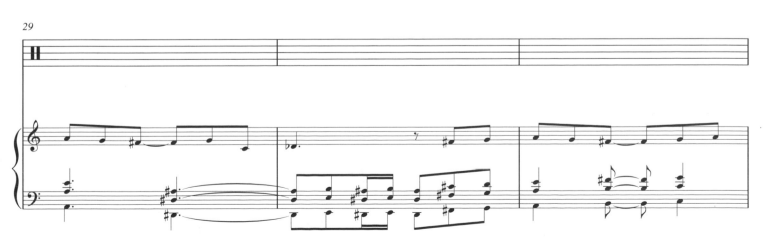

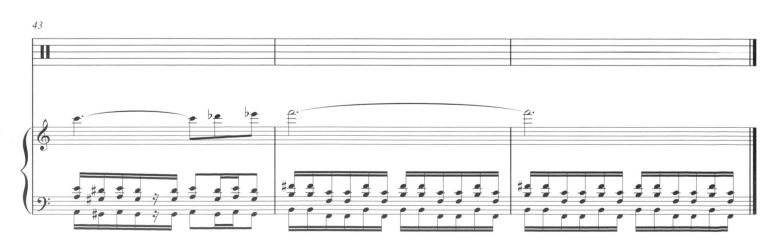

Quintuple Bypass

"Quintuple Bypass," Play-Along

The Cool Northern Sun

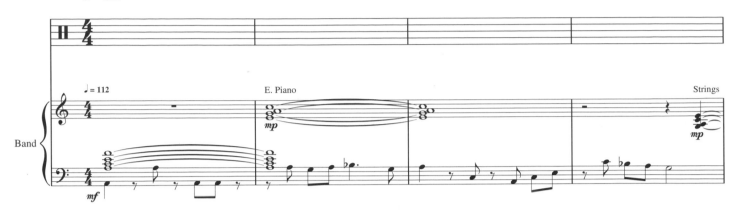 "The Cool Northern Sun," Play-Along

♩ = 112

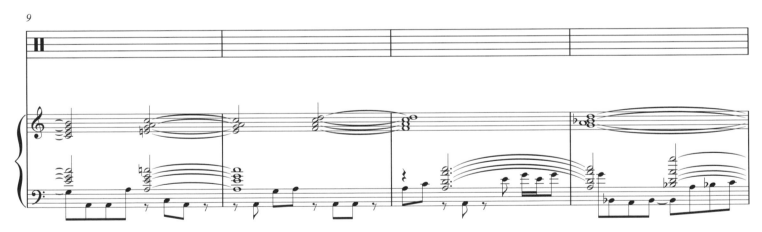

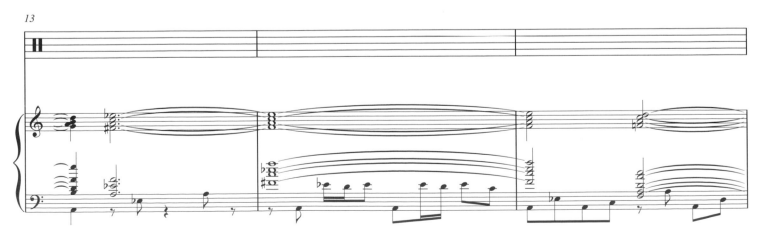

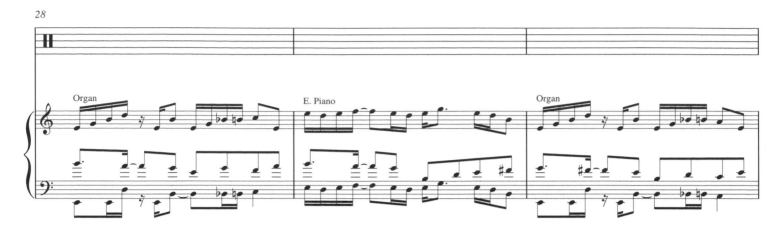

Am I Awake?

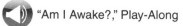
"Am I Awake?," Play-Along

Mind Control

"Mind Control," Play-Along

♩. = 92

Mad Science

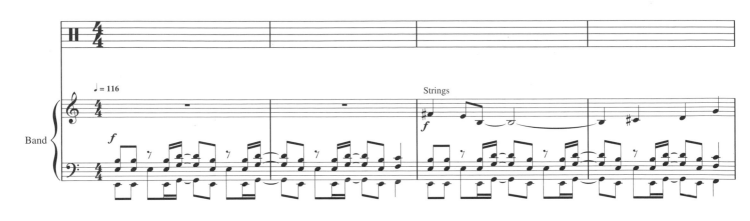

"Mad Science," Play-Along

♩ = 116

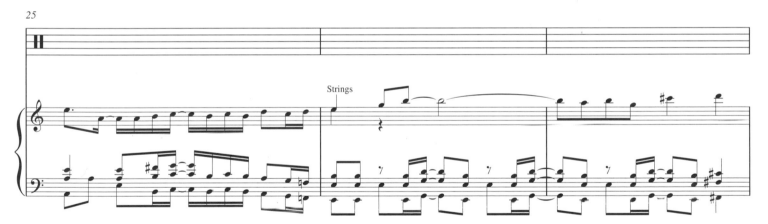

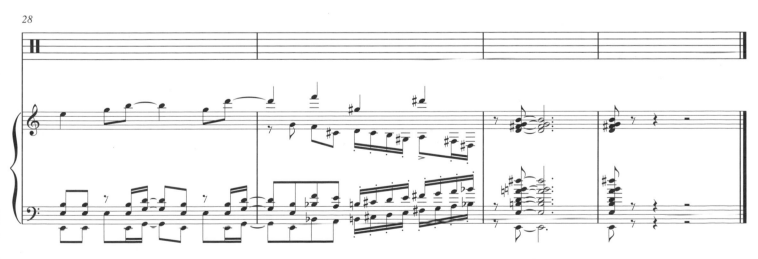

Below Zero

$\quad$ ♩ = 112

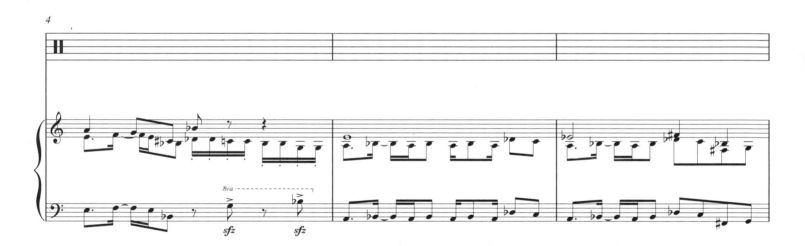

Sky Blade

"Sky Blade," Play-Along

♩ = 104

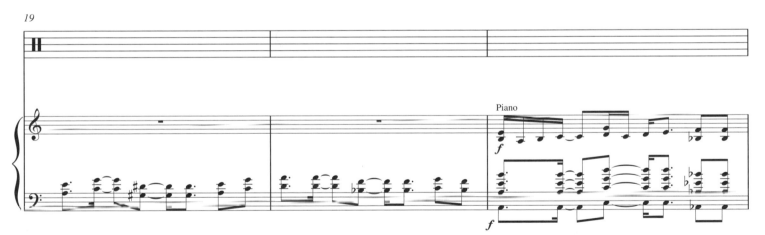

Cyborg Sleeper

"Cyborg Sleeper," Play-Along

♩ = 160

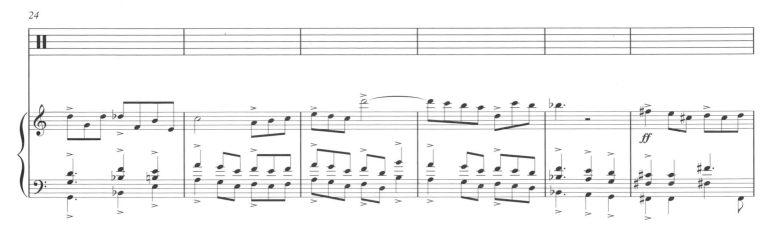

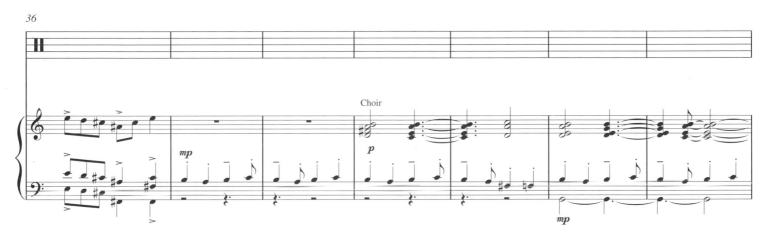

HAL·LEONARD DRUM PLAY-ALONG

Play your favorite songs quickly and easily with the *Drum Play-Along*™ series. Just follow the drum notation, listen to the CD to hear how the drums should sound, then play along using the separate backing tracks. The lyrics are also included for quick reference. The audio CD is playable on any CD player. For PC and Mac computer users, the CD is enhanced so you can adjust the recording to any tempo without changing the pitch!

1. Pop/Rock
Hurts So Good • Message in a Bottle • No Reply at All • Owner of a Lonely Heart • Peg • Rosanna • Separate Ways (Worlds Apart) • Swingtown.
00699742 Book/CD Pack.............................$12.95

2. Classic Rock
Barracuda • Come Together • Mississippi Queen • Radar Love • Space Truckin' • Walk This Way • White Room • Won't Get Fooled Again.
00699741 Book/CD Pack.............................$12.95

3. Hard Rock
Bark at the Moon • Detroit Rock City • Living After Midnight • Panama • Rock You like a Hurricane • Run to the Hills • Smoke on the Water • War Pigs (Interpolating Luke's Wall).
00699743 Book/CD Pack.............................$12.95

4. Modern Rock
Chop Suey! • Duality • Here to Stay • Judith • Nice to Know You • Nookie • One Step Closer • Whatever.
00699744 Book/CD Pack.............................$12.95

5. Funk
Cissy Strut • Cold Sweat, Part 1 • Fight the Power, Part 1 • Flashlight • Pick Up the Pieces • Shining Star • Soul Vaccination • Superstition.
00699745 Book/CD Pack.............................$14.99

6. '90s Rock
Alive • Been Caught Stealing • Cherub Rock • Give It Away • I'll Stick Around • Killing in the Name • Shine • Smells Like Teen Spirit.
00699746 Book/CD Pack.............................$14.99

7. Punk Rock
All the Small Things • Brain Stew (The Godzilla Remix) • Buddy Holly • Dirty Little Secret • Fat Lip • Flavor of the Weak • Lifestyles of the Rich and Famous • Self Esteem.
00699747 Book/CD Pack.............................$14.99

8. '80s Rock
Cult of Personality • Heaven's on Fire • Rock of Ages • Shake Me • Smokin' in the Boys Room • Talk Dirty to Me • We're Not Gonna Take It • You Give Love a Bad Name.
00699832 Book/CD Pack.............................$12.95

9. Big Band
Christopher Columbus • Corner Pocket • Flying Home • In the Mood • Opus One • Stompin' at the Savoy • Take the "A" Train • Woodchopper's Ball.
00699833 Book/CD Pack.............................$12.99

10. blink-182
Adam's Song • All the Small Things • Dammit • Feeling This • Man Overboard • The Rock Show • Stay Together for the Kids • What's My Age Again?
00699834 Book/CD Pack.............................$14.95

11. Jimi Hendrix Experience: Smash Hits
All Along the Watchtower • Can You See Me? • Crosstown Traffic • Fire • Foxey Lady • Hey Joe • Manic Depression • Purple Haze • Red House • Remember • Stone Free • The Wind Cries Mary.
00699835 Book/CD Pack.............................$16.95

12. The Police
Can't Stand Losing You • De Do Do Do, De Da Da Da • Don't Stand So Close to Me • Every Breath You Take • Every Little Thing She Does Is Magic • Spirits in the Material World • Synchronicity II • Walking on the Moon.
00700268 Book/CD Pack.............................$14.99

13. Steely Dan
Deacon Blues • Do It Again • FM • Hey Nineteen • Josie • My Old School • Reeling in the Years.
00700202 Book/CD Pack.............................$16.99

15. Lennon & McCartney
Back in the U.S.S.R. • Day Tripper • Drive My Car • Get Back • A Hard Day's Night • Paperback Writer • Revolution • Ticket to Ride.
00700271 Book/CD Pack.............................$14.99

17. Nirvana
About a Girl • All Apologies • Come As You Are • Dumb • Heart Shaped Box • In Bloom • Lithium • Smells like Teen Spirit.
00700273 Book/CD Pack.............................$14.95

18. Motown
Ain't Too Proud to Beg • Dancing in the Street • Get Ready • How Sweet It Is (To Be Loved by You) • I Can't Help Myself (Sugar Pie, Honey Bunch) • Sir Duke • Stop! in the Name of Love • You've Really Got a Hold on Me.
00700274 Book/CD Pack.............................$12.99

19. Rock Band: Modern Rock Edition
Are You Gonna Be My Girl • Black Hole Sun • Creep • Dani California • In Bloom • Learn to Fly • Say It Ain't So • When You Were Young.
00700707 Book/CD Pack.............................$14.95

20. Rock Band: Classic Rock Edition
Ballroom Blitz • Detroit Rock City • Don't Fear the Reaper • Gimme Shelter • Highway Star • Mississippi Queen • Suffragette City • Train Kept A-Rollin'.
00700708 Book/CD Pack.............................$14.95

21. Weezer
Beverly Hills • Buddy Holly • Dope Nose • Hash Pipe • My Name Is Jonas • Pork and Beans • Say It Ain't So • Undone – The Sweater Song.
00700959 Book/CD Pack.............................$14.99

22. Black Sabbath
Children of the Grave • Iron Man • N.I.B. • Paranoid • Sabbath, Bloody Sabbath • Sweet Leaf • War Pigs (Interpolating Luke's Wall).
00701190 Book/CD Pack.............................$16.99

23. The Who
Baba O'Riley • Bargain • Behind Blue Eyes • The Kids Are Alright • Long Live Rock • Pinball Wizard • The Seeker • Won't Get Fooled Again.
00701191 Book/CD Pack.............................$16.99

24. Pink Floyd – Dark Side of the Moon
Any Colour You Like • Brain Damage • Breathe • Eclipse • Money • Time • Us and Them.
00701612 Book/CD Pack.............................$14.99

25. Bob Marley
Could You Be Loved • Get Up Stand Up • I Shot the Sheriff • Is This Love • Jamming • No Woman No Cry • Stir It Up • Three Little Birds • Waiting in Vain.
00701703 Book/CD Pack.............................$14.99

26. Aerosmith
Back in the Saddle • Draw the Line • Dream On • Last Child • Mama Kin • Same Old Song and Dance • Sweet Emotion • Walk This Way.
00701887 Book/CD Pack.............................$14.99

27. Modern Worship
Beautiful One • Days of Elijah • Hear Our Praises • Holy Is the Lord • How Great Is Our God • I Give You My Heart • Worthy Is the Lamb • You Are Holy (Prince of Peace).
00701921 Book/CD Pack.............................$12.99

28. Avenged Sevenfold
Afterlife • Almost Easy • Bat Country • Beast and the Harlot • Nightmare • Scream • Unholy Confessions.
00702388 Book/CD Pack.............................$17.99

31. Red Hot Chili Peppers
The Adventures of Rain Dance Maggie • By the Way • Californication • Can't Stop • Dani California • Scar Tissue • Suck My Kiss • Tell Me Baby • Under the Bridge.
00702992 Book/CD Pack.............................$19.99

32. Songs for Beginners
Another One Bites the Dust • Billie Jean • Green River • Helter Skelter • I Won't Back Down • Living After Midnight • The Reason • 21 Guns.
00704204 Book/CD Pack.............................$14.99

HAL·LEONARD® CORPORATION
7777 W. BLUEMOUND RD. P.O. BOX 13819 MILWAUKEE, WI 53213

Visit Hal Leonard Online at
www.halleonard.com

0414

YOU CAN'T BEAT OUR DRUM BOOKS!

Learn to Play the Drumset – Book 1
by Peter Magadini
This unique method starts students out on the entire drumset and teaches them the basics in the shortest amount of time. Book 1 covers basic 4- and 5-piece set-ups, grips and sticks, reading and improvisation, coordination of hands and feet, and features a variety of contemporary and basic rhythm patterns with exercise breakdowns for each.
06620030 Book/CD Pack... $14.99

Creative Timekeeping For The Contemporary Jazz Drummer
by Rick Mattingly
Combining a variety of jazz ride cymbal patterns with coordination and reading exercises, *Creative Timekeeping* develops true independence: the ability to play any rhythm on the ride cymbal while playing any rhythm on the snare and bass drums. It provides a variety of jazz ride cymbal patterns as well as coordination and reading exercises that can be played along with them. Five chapters: Ride Cymbal Patterns; Coordination Patterns and Reading; Combination Patterns and Reading; Applications; and Cymbal Reading.
06621764 .... $8.95

The Drumset Musician
by Rod Morgenstein and Rick Mattingly
Containing hundreds of practical, usable beats and fills, The Drumset Musician teaches you how to apply a variety of patterns and grooves to the actual performance of songs. The accompanying CD includes demos as well as 14 play-along tracks covering a wide range of rock, blues and pop styles, with detailed instructions on how to create exciting, solid drum parts.
06620011 Book/CD Pack... $19.99

Drum Aerobics
by Andy Ziker
A 52-week, one-exercise-per-day workout program for developing, improving, and maintaining drum technique. Players of all levels – beginners to advanced – will increase their speed, coordination, dexterity and accuracy. The two CDs contain all 365 workout licks, plus play-along grooves in styles including rock, blues, jazz, heavy metal, reggae, funk, calypso, bossa nova, march, mambo, New Orleans 2nd Line, and lots more!
06620137 Book/2-CD Pack $19.99

40 Intermediate Snare Drum Solos
For Concert Performance
by Ben Hans
This book provides the advancing percussionist with interesting solo material in all musical styles. It is designed as a lesson supplement, or as performance material for recitals and solo competitions. Includes: 40 intermediate snare drum solos presented in easy-to-read notation; a music glossary; Percussive Arts Society rudiment chart; suggested sticking, dynamics and articulation markings; and much more!
06620067 .... $7.99

Joe Porcaro's Drumset Method – Groovin' with Rudiments
Patterns Applied to Rock, Jazz & Latin Drumset
by Joe Porcaro
Master teacher Joe Porcaro presents rudiments at the drumset in this sensational new edition of *Groovin' with Rudiments*. This book is chock full of exciting drum grooves, sticking patterns, fills, polyrhythmic adaptations, odd meters, and fantastic solo ideas in jazz, rock, and Latin feels. The enclosed CD features 99 audio clip examples in many styles to round out this true collection of superb drumming material for every serious drumset performer.
06620129 Book/CD Pack.. $24.99

Show Drumming
The Essential Guide to Playing Drumset for Live Shows and Musicals
by Ed Shaughnessy and Clem DeRosa
Who better to teach you than "America's Premier Showdrummer" himself, Mr. Ed Shaughnessy! Features: a step-by-step walk-through of a simulated show; CD with music, comments & tips from Ed; notated examples; practical tips; advice on instruments; a special accessories section with photos; and more!
06620080 Book/CD Pack... $16.95

Instant Guide to Drum Grooves
The Essential Reference for the Working Drummer
by Maria Martinez
Become a more versatile drumset player! From traditional Dixieland to cutting-edge hip-hop, Instant Guide to Drum Grooves is a handy source featuring 100 patterns that will prepare working drummers for the stylistic variety of modern gigs. The book includes essential beats and grooves in such styles as: jazz, shuffle, country, rock, funk, New Orleans, reggae, calypso, Brazilian and Latin.
06620056 Book/CD Pack... $9.95

The Complete Drumset Rudiments
by Peter Magadini
Use your imagination to incorporate these rudimental etudes into new patterns that you can apply to the drumset or tom toms as you develop your hand technique with the Snare Drum Rudiments, your hand and foot technique with the Drumset Rudiments and your polyrhythmic technique with the Polyrhythm Rudiments. Adopt them all into your own creative expressions based on ideas you come up with while practicing.
06620016 Book/CD Pack... $14.95

Drum Tuning
The Ultimate Guide
by Scott Schroedl
This book/CD pack is designed for drummers of all styles and levels. It contains step-by-step instruction along with over 35 professional photos that allow you to see the tools and tuning techniques up close. Covers: preparation; drumhead basics; drum construction and head properties; tom-toms; snare drum; bassdrum; the drum set as one instrument; drum sounds and tuning over the years; when to change heads; and more.
06620060 Book/CD Pack... $14.95

FOR MORE INFORMATION, SEE YOUR LOCAL MUSIC DEALER, OR WRITE TO:

HAL•LEONARD® CORPORATION
7777 W. BLUEMOUND RD. P.O. BOX 13819 MILWAUKEE, WI 53213

Prices, contents, and availability subject to change without notice.

www.halleonard.com

0713